AF761427

RECURRING ECONOMIC CRISIS IN KOREA

RECURRING ECONOMIC CRISIS IN KOREA

JONG KYU LEE
AND
SANGHACK LEE

Nova Science Publishers, Inc.
New York

For permission to use material from this book please contact us:
Telephone 631-231-7269; Fax 631-231-8175
Web Site: http://www.novapublishers.com

LIBRARY OF CONGRESS CATALOGING-IN-PUBLICATION DATA

Lee, Jong Kyu, 1957-
Recurring economic crisis in Korea / Jong Kyu Lee and Sanghack Lee.
p. cm.
Includes bibliographical references and index.
ISBN 978-1-60456-188-3 (hardcover)
1. Korea (South)--Economic conditions--1960- 2. Financial crises--Korea (South) 3. Structural adjustment (Economic policy)--Korea (South) I. Lee, Sanghack. II. Title.
HC467.95.L435 007
330.95195'043--dc22 2007045021

Published by Nova Science Publishers, Inc. ✦ New York

CONTENTS

PREFACE

There exists a large volume of literature on Korean success in economic development. However, Korea has experienced several economic crises in the development process. While the financial crisis in 1997 has received substantial amount of attention in the mass media and in the academic as well, Korea had not been immune to economic crisis prior to the 1997 financial crisis. This book reviews the experiences of economic crises and their resolutions in Korea since 1960s. The book examines each crisis and finds out that the factors that caused one previous crisis later brought about another crisis repeatedly. This indicates that the measures to resolve the previous crises were ultimately ineffective in the sense that the fundamental causes for the economic crisis had remained unresolved and, as a result, recurrence of the crisis has not been prevented. Most of the past crisis resolution measures were focused on disposing of the losses incurred by firms and banks through such instruments as bail-out loans. Stabilization measures were adopted just when the economy had begun to stagnate after a long period of boom, and seldom contributed to preventing recurrence of crisis; they rather amplified the intensity of the crisis. These results contain lessons for the current and future structural adjustment policy, to be adopted as a means to prevent recurrence of economic crisis. First, it should be designed in such a way as to encourage private agents to take initiative, with the government abstaining from direct intervention such as bail-out loans. This would eventually strengthen private sector capacities to overcome adverse shocks. Second, stabilization policies should be implemented in such a preemptive manner that they can prevent an exceptional boom or wide-spread speculation.

Keywords: Korea, Economic Crisis, Crisis Resolution, Structural Adjustment, Macroeconomic Policy, Economic History of Korea.

ACKNOWLEDGEMENTS

The authors would like to thank their colleagues for their constructive comments and suggestions. This book is a substantially revised version of the working paper entitled "Korean Experiences of Economic Crisis Resolution" by the first author. The views contained in this paper are the authors' own, and do not necessarily represent the official views of the Bank of Korea.

ABOUT THE AUTHORS

Jong Kyu Lee is a Chief Economist at the Institute for Monetary and Economic Research, The Bank of Korea, Tel: +82-2-759-5412, Fax: +82-2-759-5410, e-mail: jonglee@bok.or.kr

Sanghack Lee is a Professor of Economics at the School of Economics, Kookmin University. He is also the corresponding author for this book. Address: School of Economics, Kookmin University, Seoul 136-702, South Korea. Tel.: +82-2-910-4546, Fax: +82-2-910-4519, e-mail: slee@kookmin.ac.kr

Chapter 1

INTRODUCTION

There exists a large volume of literature on Korean[1] success in economic development. However, it should be noted that Korea has also experienced several economic crises in the development process. While the financial crisis in 1997 has received huge amount of attention in the mass media and in the academic as well, Korea was not immune to economic crisis prior to 1997 financial crisis. This neglect of past economic crisis of Korea is partly attributable to spectacular performance of the Korean economy. It should, however, be noted that Korean economy had also experienced several economic crises before the 1997 crisis.

The Korean government adopted various policies or institutional devices to prevent recurrence of economic crisis since 1997. Commonly known as 'restructuring policy' or 'structural adjustment policy,' these policies aimed at preventing crisis by improving the structural efficiency of the Korean economy.

Whether such restructuring policies are on the right track, however, has been heavily disputed[2]. In light of a wide variety of criticism from various points of view, this book tries to reinterpret Korean experiences of economic crises in the past from a new viewpoint, and also tries to extract lessons for structural adjustment policies.

Most of the discussions and research on structural adjustment, now being extensively studied around the world, draw their arguments from experiences in

---

[1] Korea refers to South Korea.

[2] The set of methods for assessing the effectiveness of restructuring policy includes: ① comparing performances before and after reforms are introduced, ② comparing actual performance with reform objectives, ③ comparing the economic performance of the reforming country with those of non-reforming countries, ④ comparing the economic performances of cases of reforming and cases of not reforming through counterfactual simulation (Schandler et al., 1995).

the process of economic development, rather than from a general theoretical framework. The concept of structural adjustment was introduced by the World Bank; the World Bank came to use the term structural adjustment as it recognized, after many trials and errors, the importance of improving the efficiency of an economic system as a whole in achieving sustained growth. Since, it is practically impossible to design an ideal economic system *a priori*, any country that wants to improve the efficiency of its economic system will need to learn from its own experience, or from other countries' experiences in similar situations.

Foreign experience has only limited usefulness as a reference, however, because there are many factors specific to a country that make its experience difficult to apply to another country's structural adjustment process. In this respect, deriving lessons for a country from its own experience of structural adjustment would be more useful. Perhaps this is why, in the U.S.A., the Great Depression of 1929 is still a popular topic of research. Also, it is quite natural for one who wants to resolve a present problem to seek lessons from the past successes and failures.

Despite all the past restructuring, Korea is not immune to future economic crisis. The purpose of this research is to find out ways to enhance the effectiveness of measures for possible future economic crisis in Korea, by making use of the lessons extracted from the past economic crises Korea experienced since the launch of industrialization policy in the 1960s, and their resolutions. Even though Korea's history of economic development is relatively short, it contains several episodes of crisis worthy of thorough analysis. In particular, the experience of overcoming several crises in the past can be a valuable source of lessons useful in resolving the future crisis. Korean experience in crisis resolution as well as economic development can be a valuable asset to other countries seeking to emulate Korean economic success.

This book will look into the specifics and backgrounds of, and the policy measures undertaken to deal with four crises in Korea, and analyze the effectiveness of those policy measures. Besides the period since 1997, Korea has had several occasions of severe economic difficulties -- including the period from the late 1960s to the early 1970s, that around 1980, and that from the late 1980s to the early 1990s. By comparing the specifics of each crisis, we are able to better understand the nature of the economic crises in Korea. Further, by assessing the effects of policies to resolve the former crises, we may be better able to derive some important policy agenda for overcoming the future crisis.

The discussion will proceed keeping an eye on the causal aspects of each economic crisis: formation of bubbles, deterioration of profitability in the corporate sector, weaknesses in financial structure, maturity mismatches, and policy mistakes. This will provide a basis for comparing crises whose actual causes differed from each other in kind and in specifics.

It should also be mentioned that this book reviews critically the past experience in coping with crises. This criticism stems from the observation that the same factors that had caused a previous crisis later brought about another crisis repeatedly. For example, the factors behind the 1997 crisis were similar to those behind the past crises. This implies that the measures taken to resolve the previous crises were ultimately limited and/or ineffective.

The remainder of this paper is organized as follows. Chapter 2 starts with general discussion on the definition and causes of economic crisis. Chapter 2 then describes and analyzes the details, backgrounds, and policy responses by government to the four Korean episodes of economic crises[3]. In Chapter 3 the crisis resolution measures are assessed in terms of their effectiveness. On the basis of this, derivation of effective crisis resolution measures will be considered. In Chapter 4, the characteristics of the 1997 economic crisis are summarized, and the structural adjustment policy implemented afterwards is compared with those implemented in past cases. Finally, in the Concluding Remarks, the usefulness and limitations of this research are discussed and new research directions are suggested.

[3] The main contents of Chapter 2 and Chapter 3 are excerpted from Lee (2000). Those who are interested in details are advised to refer to Lee (2000).

Chapter 2

KOREAN EXPERIENCE IN RESOLVING ECONOMIC CRISES

1. FOUR ECONOMIC CRISES OF KOREA

An economic crisis is a situation of extreme economic difficulties, such as firms and banks going out of business one after another, the prices of goods, exchange rates, or interest rates fluctuating very rapidly, or production decreasing sharply with the unemployment rate increasing. Thus, it is sometimes treated as being equivalent to a severe recession.

This concept, however, does not give any information about the economic crisis, and is not so much helpful to theoretically grasping its systematic aspects. It is thus preferable to define an economic crisis as a situation in which exceptional responses of economic agents to unexpected economic events hamper the proper functioning of major parts of the economic system, and in extreme cases cause the whole system to collapse. In short, an economic crisis refers to a situation in which part or all of the economic system does not function normally, causing economic difficulties.

An economic system comprises various components. When all of the components combine organically and harmoniously, it works properly. When the various components do not combine harmoniously, it malfunctions. In this sense, an economic crisis is a kind of coordination failure -- one especially severe in nature.

The term "economic crisis" carries a strong negative connotation since the phenomenon itself brings economic suffering to many people. It also has a positive aspect, however, because economic problems which need to be addressed reveal themselves in a crisis. For instance, economic crisis tends to occur when an economy suffers from difficulties in adapting itself to a changed environment; once it occurs, the part of the economic system which has been unable to adapt is revealed. Therefore, an economic crisis also plays the positive role of informing policy makers and the general public of what the fundamental weaknesses of the system are, thus providing an opportunity for an economy to correct them and prosper again.

In the course of economic development, an economy faces significant changes in its economic environment. Sometimes, it adapts itself to them successfully. Sometimes, it fails. In the latter case, a crisis or a crisis-like situation takes place. In this sense, economic crisis represents the adaptive failure of an economy. Finally, an economic crisis, though it is exceptional and unique, is a universal phenomenon that can happen to any economy in any phase of development.

The factors leading to economic crises, as identified in the literature, are summarized in Table 1. This list is not intended to be exhaustive; there are many unknown causes, as is revealed by the fact that a crisis usually comes by surprise.

There are two kinds of theories for explaining the factors behind an economic crisis[1]. One pertains to the causes for an economic crisis and the other to the propagation mechanism of an economic crisis. Business cycle theories, monetarists' views, the financial instability hypothesis, and microeconomic finance theories are examples of the former. The views that attribute an economic crisis to policy failures, or to failure in internal risk control, also belong to this type of theory. On the other hand, contagion effects among sectors and countries, the effect of rumor, and the crisis-hit economy's loss of ability to restore equilibrium are the main building blocks of the latter type of theory. Therefore, it would be reasonable to mention two different sets of causes of economic crisis, in accordance with the two theories. Nevertheless, Table 1 lists the causes of economic crisis drawn from the first type of theory alone, since these causes seem to be applicable in case of economic crisis propagation as well.

Table 1 does not include shocks external to an economy as a cause of economic crises. The reason is mainly because this book aims at *deriving lessons* from the experience discussed; in other words, recognition of external shocks as the cause of a crisis does not lead to a meaningful answer to the question: what should we do to prevent another crisis? Therefore, it is preferred here to recognize

[1] One of the reasons why there are few studies of economic crisis is that the mainstream economics have considered it too exceptional or abnormal a phenomenon to fit into their equilibrium model framework.

internal vulnerabilities as the main cause of crisis. On the basis of this approach, the table focuses on causes of economic fragility[2].

Table 1. Factors Behind Economic Crises

Theory		Causes
Business Cycles		macroeconomic disequilibrium: over-investment, under-consumption discrepancy between monetary and natural(real) interest rates misperception or incorrect forecast changes in profit rate
Monetarist		banking panic
Financial Instability Hypothesis		bubbles: speculative mania
Micro-finance Theory	Intrinsic Factors	imperfect information information asymmetry nature of debt contracts asset specificity herd behavior "me-first" tendency
	Immediate Causes	deterioration of profitability financial fragility maturity mismatches bubbles
Others		policy failures failures in internal risk control

Among various factors listed, the table refers to intrinsic factors behind an economic crisis, including imperfect information, herd behavior, and so on. These are hard to eliminate since they are intrinsic to human nature or the capitalist economic system. Thus, in cases where these factors are the main cause of a crisis, it would be hard to cure that crisis fundamentally. This is why herd behavior, though frequently blamed as the culprit, is seldom studied in depth. Unlike the case with external shocks, research on intrinsic factors can provide significant clues to understanding the process of economic development since the

[2] In what follows are arguments that attribute the past economic crises in Korea to worsening world economic environments. However, this is not so much to identify the external shocks as the causes of the crisis as to represent the economic recession or deterioration of profits indirectly by it.

history of economic development can be said to have been a process of overcoming the limits imposed by these factors. Thus, a systematic study of an economic crisis will show the ways to long-term economic development as well as crisis resolution. This theme, however, is beyond the scope of this paper. This book will focus on the immediate causes of economic crisis, such as deterioration of profitability, financial fragility, maturity mismatches, and bubbles.

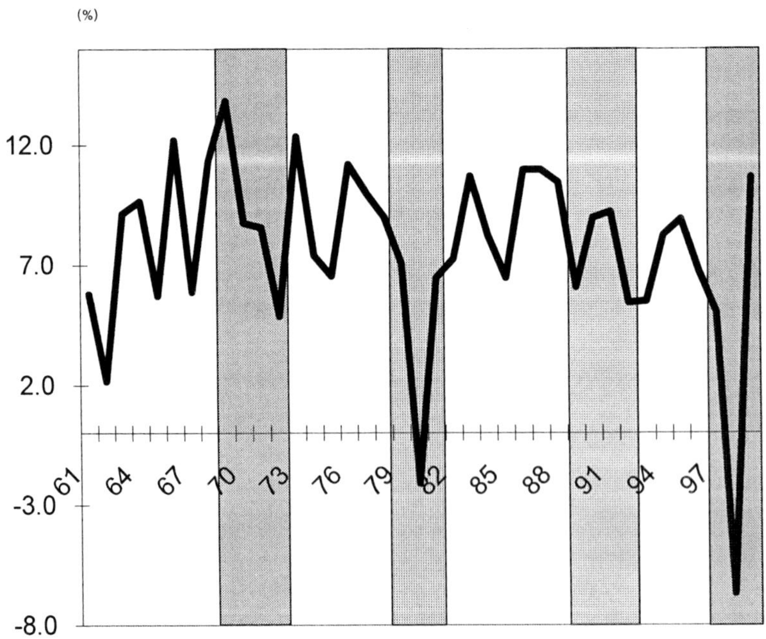

Note: The shaded areas indicate the periods of economic crises.
Source: The Bank of Korea, *Economic Statistics Yearbook*, various issues

Figure 1. Growth Rates of GDP: Four Crisis Periods

Based on the general understanding of the causes for an economic crisis and the measures for coping with it, we can identify four economic crises in Korea. There have been four crises[3], or similar situations, since the year 1962, when the first five-year economic development plan began. The first economic crisis took place during the period from the late 1960s to the early 1970s; it was

[3] Here, an economic crisis is seen simply as a severe economic difficulty or economically critical situation.

characterized by high inflation, large and expanding current account deficits in the wake of the late 1960s economic boom, snowballing foreign debts, decreasing business profits, deteriorating financial soundness of firms, and impending large scale business failures in the early 1970s. The second crisis, around 1980, came about in the wake of the second global oil shock, soaring international interest rates, political unrest, and a bad harvest. Production literally decreased, and the foreign debt situation was so bad that the country could not repay some of them. The third crisis, during the period from the late 1980s to the early 1990s, was called a "critical situation on the whole." It followed deterioration in the international competitiveness of domestic firms, over-consumption and speculative bubbles on assets such as real estate. The fourth crisis, finally, happened in 1997. It was accompanied by serial bankruptcy of large business firms and increases in non-performing loans at financial institutions. Figure 1 depicts the growth rates of GDP since the 1960s and the economic crises in Korea.

2. The 1972 Economic Crisis

A. Unfolding of the Crisis[4]

The Korean economy faced a crisis in the early 1970s after an investment boom in the late 1960s, corresponding to the first half period of the second 5-year economic development plan. Investment stagnated three years in a row, from 1970 on (refer to table 2). Apparently, economic growth rates were not so bad. However, capital formation plummeted, casting doubt on future growth potential. Current account also deteriorated. It seems that not only the government's economic stabilization policy, which began around the end of 1969, but also the worsening of the firms' debt-servicing burdens contributed to the stagnation of business investment; firms could not expand their production capacity since they were under strong pressure to repay debts that had accumulated to very risky levels during the previous boom period. The stagnation of investment was a critical obstacle to the government's ambitious economic development plan to develop the heavy and chemical industries.

Moreover, the number of delinquent firms had increased since the economic recession that began around 1969; many firms could not repay their foreign loans, which were guaranteed by domestic banks. The third-party banks' repayments of

[4] This explanation of the 1972 economic crisis is largely based on Kim (1990).

the foreign debt amounted to 0.5 billion Won in March 1970, and increased to 2.3 billion Won in August 1971[5]. The increase in business delinquencies might have been affected by the worsening profitability of firms due to the downturn of the business cycle. But the most important factor was the huge debt-servicing burden. The foreign loans that had been raised in large amounts in the late 1960s were reaching maturity. The burden had been further exacerbated by the Won depreciation, from 271.20 Won to 304.35 Won per US dollar in November 1969, and again to 370.80 won in June 1971.

Table 2. Trends of Major Economic Indicators up to 1972

	1967	1968	1969	1970	1971	1972
Economic Growth[1)](%)	5.9	11.3	13.8	8.8	8.6	4.9
(manufacturing)	21.6	27.2	21.6	19.9	18.5	14.3
Consumption	8.3	9.6	9.4	9.5	8.2	4.6
Capital formation	22.6	37.4	24.8	1.0	3.0	1.2
Exports	32.7	39.5	36.1	19.6	21.5	37.5
Imports	30.8	43.6	26.6	8.0	19.2	0.7
Current Account (100mil. USD)	-1.9	-4.4	-5.5	-6.2	-8.5	-3.7
WPI(rate of change, %)	6.5	8.1	6.9	9.4	8.6	13.8
CPI(rate of change, %)	10.9	10.8	12.8	15.5	13.5	11.7
M_2(end of year, rate of change, %)	61.7	72.0	61.4	27.4	20.8	33.8
Budget Balance[2)]/GDP(%)	-2.57	-1.83	-3.10	-1.88	-1.70	-5.01

Note: 1) Growth rates of GDP are on the basis of 1975 prices up to 1970 and thereafter on the basis of 1995 prices.
2) Only the budget of central government is included.
Source: The Bank of Korea, *Economic Statistics Yearbook*, various issues.

By 1969, the government had recognized the seriousness of the situation and launched an operation to liquidate insolvent firms, by establishing an insolvent-firm liquidation unit under direct control of the president. In May 1969, this unit designated 30 foreign debt laden firms and 56 firms under bank control as insolvent[6].

---

5 The size of M_1 was about 300 billion won, and that of M_2 was about 900 billion won at the end of 1970.

6 The unit was later succeeded by the corporation rationalization commission which took over the job of liquidation of troubled firms.

The government was eventually forced to resort to an emergency decree on August 3rd, 1972, in consideration of the several factors as follows. First, the government perceived it difficult to let many delinquent firms go bankrupt because they were too big to fail and they were also greatly indebted to foreign banks, and their bankruptcies would have triggered a rush by international lenders to collect loans, and at the same time made them unwilling to provide new loans. Once this happened, the Korean economy would have faced severe difficulties in financing its economic development plan for the heavy and chemical industries since domestic savings were very limited in those days.

Second, policy makers began to worry that the firms' weak financial positions might bring about a disaster for firms and banks; the increase in the number of delinquent firms posed a potential threat to the banking system due to the increase in non-performing loans. Moreover, since the government had just started its campaign for heavy and chemical industrialization, the weak financial structures of the major firms were also perceived as a threat to the government's vision of economic development through active investment in those industries.

Finally, the booming curb money market was suspected as one of the main culprits behind the increasing number of corporate insolvency. Curb market lenders collected their loans whenever the borrowers were known to have difficulties in debt-servicing, ignoring the implicit maturities of the loans. The curb markets were thought to have other adverse effects on the economy as well, such as providing tax loopholes and disturbing the orderly operation of the financial system. On these grounds, the government issued the August 3rd Decree, aiming at improving corporate financial structure.

Thus, the early 1970s economic crisis was a corporate crisis in nature; that is, the primary source of the crisis was corporate insolvencies. Such factors as foreign debts, a slowdown in economic growth, and inflation were only secondary.

B. Background of the Crisis

(1) A Boom Financed by High Leverage – Rent Seeking through Financial Regulation

In the background of the worsening corporate financial positions lay the investment boom in the late 1960s, which was financed by ever-increasing leverage. Following the interest rate liberalization measures in September 30, 1965, monetary aggregates expanded rapidly (refer to Table 2). Together with this, the economy began to grow at more than 10 percent a year, with business investment growth averaging 28.3 percent a year during the period from 1967 to 1969. Lacking internal funds, however, domestic firms had to rely on external funds, especially bank loans. This implied that the faster the economy grew, the larger the borrowings of the firms, and the more vulnerable the firms would be to external shocks. This was what happened to Korean firms in the late 1960s. The debt-equity ratio of Korean manufacturing increased from 93.7 percent in 1965 to 394.2 percent in 1971. The financial expenses-to-sales ratio increased, accordingly, from 3.91 to 9.86 percent during the same period.

Table 3. Financial Indicators of Korean Manufacturing Industry (%)

	1965	1966	1967	1968	1969	1970	1971	1972
Debt-equity ratio	93.7	117.7	151.2	201.3	270.0	328.4	394.2	313.4
Financial expenses-sales ratio	3.91	5.65	5.19	5.90	7.81	9.15	9.86	7.08
Net income-assets ratio	7.9	7.8	6.7	5.4	3.6	0.9	0.9	3.8

Source: The Bank of Korea, *Financial Statements Analysis,* various issues.

The high rate of return on investment in real assets, along with rapid economic growth, augmented corporations' ever-increasing demand for borrowing. A development boom raised the prices of real estate in several regions, and speculative investments boosted them further to extremely high levels. This produced a situation in which the gap between the rate of return in the real sector and that in the financial sector never narrowed. Even though the sum of the growth rates of GDP and the consumer price index, which was 22.3 percent on average during the period from 1967 to 1971, was lower than the lending rate for general funds, at 24.2 percent a year, the rate of return in the real sector is believed to have exceeded that in the financial sector because the levels of prices of many products were under strong government control. Moreover, considering the lending rates for policy loans such as equipment funds, the borrowing costs of firms seem to have been no more than half of their rates of return on investment.

Table 4. Interest Rates and Related Indices (%)

	1965	1966	1967	1968	1969	1970	1971	1972
Interest rate on commercial bill discounts[1)]	24.0	24.0	24.0	26.0	24.6	24.0	22.0	15.5
Interest rate on equipment funds[2)]	11.5	11.5	11.5	11.5	12.0	12.0	12.0	10.0
Economic growth rate(A)	5.7	12.2	5.9	11.3	13.8	8.8	8.6	4.9
Rate of change in CPI [3)](B)	13.5	11.2	10.9	10.8	12.8	15.5	13.5	11.7
A+B	19.2	23.4	16.7	21.7	26.7	24.4	22.1	16.4

Note: 1) Offered by deposit monetary banks as of the end of year.
2) Offered by the Industrial Bank of Korea as of the end of year.
3) The figure in 1965 is for the Seoul district, and figures in 1966 and thereafter for all cities.
Source: The Bank of Korea, *Economic Statistics Yearbook*, various issues.

(2) Underdevelopment of the Financial System

As a further background cause of the crisis, it can be pointed out that the financial system then was so backward that bank loans were almost the only source of external funds for most firms. The financial markets were segmented into a formal one and an informal one. Securities markets were in such an inactive state that they could be said to have been almost non-existent. There were several reasons for this. Firstly, the stock market was sluggish after a scandalous boom and bust in the early 1960s; secondly, expectation of inflation remained at a high level, which discouraged long-term investments in securities. Also, with most firms in their early stages of development and thus not proven to be creditworthy, fund raising through new issues of equity in the capital market was an unrealistic option. Thus, the increased demand for funds was mostly met by bank loans, and the excess demand for bank loans was spilled over to the curb markets.

The distortion in financial parameters, a side-effect of the measures liberalizing interest rates in 1965, encouraged firms to borrow excessively and thus led them to suffer from excessive debt service burdens. As a result of the policy of keeping interest rates on policy loans at lower-than-the-market level, the loan-deposit interest rate spread became negative. This created excessive speculative demand for funds, thus distorting orderly operation of the financial system, and eventually resulting in the underdevelopment of the Korean financial system.[7]

---

[7] Lee and Cheong (2007) offer an empirical and theoretical analysis for the political economy of financial structure of Korean firms. They argue that financial markets are repressed to create rent, which were shared by politicians and business sectors. Kang (2002) also provides a related research on this issue.

(3) Adverse Effects of Economic Stabilization Policy

In the latter half of the 1960s, various signs of an overheating economy such as widening current account deficits and soaring prices emerged. The government, therefore, executed a comprehensive stabilization policy in November 1969[8]. However, this aggravated the difficulties of most firms, which had weakness in their financial structure. The main contents of the stabilization policy were regulation of private borrowing from abroad, tightening of government expenditures, control of the money supply, and so on (The Bank of Korea 2000, pp. 166). In particular, the Bank of Korea changed the monetary policy regime, from indirect monetary targeting to direct control of the domestic credits of financial institutions from 1970 on. In the meantime, as the economy cooled down, the Bank of Korea lowered the interest rates, which had been at excessively high levels since the interest rate rationalization in 1965.

The firms over-laden with large debts and their debt-servicing costs went to the curb market for funds when their access to financial institutions and foreign loans were limited. Because the interest rate in the curb market then climbed to and maintained levels higher than 3~4 percent a month (over 40 percent a year), the firms' financial burdens increased all the more. Furthermore, the risks of bankruptcy of firms increased as the economy marched into recession.

(4) Worsened World Economic Situation

Economic stagnation in advanced countries, in the wake of the breakdown of the old international monetary system (the Bretton-Woods system), also aggravated the difficulties of Korean firms, along with the domestic business slowdown. The United States found it difficult to maintain a fixed exchange rate for the dollar with its increasing current account and fiscal deficits. Thus, the U.S. suspended the convertibility of the dollar to gold and devalued it in 1971. As major industrial economies also adopted floating exchange rate systems, international financial markets became more volatile and the world economy subsequently began to stagnate. Influenced by this, the growth rate of Korean exports slowed down and, accordingly, profitability of the firms decreased. As a result, the firms' burdens of debt servicing worsened.

---

[8] This measure was encouraged in part by the IMF.

C. Crisis Resolution Measures

As the economy began to stagnate in early 1971, the government adopted a loose monetary policy stance, reversing the 1969 stabilization policy by lowering the interest rate and devaluing the Won on June 28th, 1971. In addition, a series of policy measures to boost the economy were adopted in February 1972. In spite of these policy measures, the firms continued to suffer, and the government finally promulgated the 'Emergency Decree for Economic Stability and Growth' on August 2nd, 1972, to come into effect on the following day.

The substance of the August 3rd Emergency Decree included above all rescheduling of the loans borrowed from the curb market as well as the banks (including the conversion of debts into capital) and promotion of policies boosting the economy. With a view to alleviating the debt-servicing burdens of firms, all reported curb-market borrowings were mandated to be converted to a new debt contract, with a three-year grace period followed by repayment in five annual installments at the interest rate of 1.35 percent a month or 16.2 percent a year. In addition, 30 percent of the outstanding short-term bank loans were rescheduled as long-term loans. A portion of the losses to financial institutions incurred by this was compensated for by support from the Bank of Korea. At the same time, the Bank of Korea lowered banks' lending and deposit rates to levels similar to those as before the interest rate liberalization in 1965. Meanwhile, the government provided tax benefits by allowing a higher depreciation ratio for fixed assets and larger corporate income tax deductions, with the purpose of stimulating investment. After the August 3rd Emergency Decree, the government promulgated three acts to attract curb-market funds into formal financial markets - the 'Short-term Financing and Banking Act,' 'the Mutual Savings and Finance Company Act,' and the 'Credit Union Act.'

3. The 1980 Economic Crisis

A. Unfolding of the Crisis

In the period around 1980, economic difficulties arose which were more severe than other difficulties a few years earlier, such as the 1972 recession and the first oil shock in 1973~1974. After a boom period from 1976 to 1978, the gross domestic product decreased, while inflation pressure emerged, in 1980, for the first time since the beginning of the 5-year economic development plans (refer to Table 5). The principal reasons for the decline of GDP were mainly external shocks such as the soaring oil price, political and social unrest, and a bad harvest. The probability of defaults on foreign debt increased as the current account deficit widened, mainly due to the increase in expenses for oil imports. Over-investment in the heavy and chemical industries, meanwhile, was another factor driving firms and banks to become insolvent.

The 1980 crisis unfolded in the following manner. Entering the year 1979, structural problems of the Korean economy began to surface. For example, exports decreased in volume terms in 1979. This decrease in exports reflected the surge in inflation in the latter half of the 1970s, which resulted in deterioration of the export competitiveness and profitability of domestic products (The Bank of Korea, *The 1979 Annual Report*). In addition, the direct control over the exports of some products, which was intended to stabilize domestic prices, also contributed to the decrease in exports. Thus, the decrease in export volume at that time may have resulted from the structural problems of the economy, even though it was affected as well by the world recession, the second oil shock, and neo-protectionism of advanced countries.

Table 5. Trends of Major Economic Indicators circa 1980

	1975	1976	1977	1978	1979	1980	1981
Economic growth[1](%)	6.5	11.2	10.0	9.0	7.1	-2.1	6.5
(manufacturing)	12.9	23.1	14.4	20.8	9.5	-0.9	9.5
Consumption	5.6	6.8	5.2	8.1	6.3	1.1	4.7
Capital formation	7.7	21.0	28.6	34.4	9.7	-10.7	-3.7
Exports	19.3	39.1	20.9	13.8	1.0	8.6	15.7
Imports	1.9	24.7	20.9	28.0	11.8	-5.3	6.6
Current account (100mil.USD)	-18.9	-3.1	0.1	-10.9	-41.5	-53.2	-45.5
WPI(rate of change, %)	26.5	12.1	9.0	11.7	18.8	33.9	20.4
CPI(rate of change, %)	25.3	15.3	10.2	14.4	18.3	28.7	21.3
M_2(end of year, rate of change, %)	27.0	29.2	37.0	39.3	26.8	25.8	27.4
Budget balance[2]/GDP(%)	-3.29	-1.13	-0.83	-0.21	0.38	-1.55	-2.22

Note: 1) Growth rates of GDP at 1995 prices

2) Only the central government budget is included.

Source: The Bank of Korea, *Economic Statistics Yearbook*, various issues.

In particular, inflation began to soar in 1979. This was mainly due to the adjustment of controlled prices to more realistic levels as well as to the increases in import prices, e.g., of crude oil. The government had been setting the maximum prices of major products since it enacted the 'Act on Price Stability' on March 12th, 1973. During the late-1970s boom, however, numerous ways to circumvent the price controls were devised, such as setting dual prices, underground transactions, refusing to sell, cornering the markets for agricultural products, and so on. As a result, the price controls became ineffective and provoked such adverse effects as distortion of resource allocation and disruption of economic order. In light of this, the government rationalized or liberalized the prices of products and fees for public utilities.

In addition to soaring inflation, the economy suffered from a severe recession in 1980 as a result of a series of external shocks such as the sudden rise in oil prices and domestic political unrest. Private investment in equipment decreased rapidly as economic uncertainty increased in the midst of low capacity utilization following excessive investment in the 1970s. Domestic demand shrank as real income decreased due to inflation and a contraction of consumer confidence. In addition, production shrank because of a poor rice harvest. As a result of this, the economic growth rate became negative and unemployment rate increased, from 3.8% in 1979 to 5.2% in 1980. The ratio of dishonored bills also increased from 0.10% in 1979 to 0.18% in 1980.

The current account, which had been in balance and once showed a surplus in 1977, turned into a large deficit in 1979 (refer to Table 6). The deficit reflected, to some degree, the structural problems in energy consumption as well as the increase in oil imports after the oil price hike.

Table 6. International Oil Prices, Interest Rates, and Total Foreign Debt

	1978	79	80	81	82
Oil Prices [a]	12.95	29.22	36.68	35.27	32.45
Interest Rate[b]	8.85	12.09	14.19	16.87	13.29
Total Foreign Debt[c]	148.2	202.9	271.7	324.3	370.8
(Net Foreign Debt)[c]	(99.0)	(139.9)	(196.3)	(244.7)	(283.0)

Notes : a) Average crude price (USD/Barrel): U.K. Brent (light), Dubai (medium), and Alaska North Slope (heavy), equally weighted.

b) Libor 3-month, %.

c) In 100 million US Dollars.

Sources: IMF, *International Financial Statistics Yearbook* (1997).

National Statistics Office, *Major Statistics of Korean Economy*, various issues.

Demand for foreign exchange began far exceeding supply as the current account was in increasingly large deficit. Meanwhile, foreign confidence in the Korean economy deteriorated as a result of the political and social unrest and the economic recession. Foreign debt turned out to be about 15 billion dollars at the end of 1978, and interest payments on this debt amounted to 0.9 billion dollars (Economic Planning Board 1985, p. 6); this was a substantial interest burden, considering the fact that the total exports of the nation were only 12 billion dollars then. Due to the large current account deficit since 1979, the country was in need of additional inflow of foreign funds. It faced difficulties in raising funds in international financial markets, however, because those markets were also in unstable situations with soaring interest rates. The country could hardly have avoided default on its foreign debt but for its drawings from the IMF funds[9]. Foreign debt continued to accumulate, however, up to 37 billion dollars at the end of 1982.

At the same time, adverse effects from the government's promotion of heavy and chemical industries began to appear. Ambitious investments in the heavy and chemical industries during the 1970s had led to duplication of investment in some industries. Domestic markets for heavy and chemical products were small, while the international competitiveness of those firms remained low. Thus, the firms that entered these industries performed poorly in terms of profitability, and it was worried that most of them would go bankrupt in the long run. Even those firms which were highly competitive could not perform well because of the world-wide economic stagnation. Moreover, it had become practically impossible to continue to channel funds to those industries, since their demand for funds was too large. For example, the demand for funds by about 40 firms in the heavy and chemical industries amounted to 80 percent of the increments in money supply that year (Economic Planning Board 1979, p. 1185). Similarly, the overseas construction companies and shipping companies, which also absorbed large investments in the latter half of the 1970s, were accumulating bad assets as well.

In short, the nature of the 1980 economic crisis was a combination of several kinds of crises. It was a macroeconomic crisis in the sense that it resulted from an external and internal disequilibrium. In particular, it was a balance of payments crisis or a foreign debt crisis since widening current account deficit and the subsequent shortage of foreign exchange supply was one of the main causes for the crisis. From the microeconomic point of view, it can be seen as a structural crisis, in the sense that it revealed the shortcomings of the economic system that

[9] The government withdrew about 500 million SDR from the IMF based on the stand-by agreement, in which Korea's credits were increased from 20 million SDR to 649 million SDR.

had prevailed in Korea during the 1970s. It also had the characteristics of a corporate crisis and a banking crisis, because of the delinquencies of the heavy and chemical industry firms and the financial distress imposed thereby on banks.

B. Background of the Crisis

(1) Over-heating and Speculation

The direct causes for the deterioration in the domestic firms' competitiveness in the export markets were an over-heated economy, during the 1976~ 1978 period, and an accompanying speculative rally in asset markets. Thanks in part to the measures contained in the 1972 August 3rd Decree to stimulate business activities, and also in part to the stabilized oil prices since 1975, the Korean economy recorded high growth rates of around 10 percent on average during the 1976~ 1978 period. Exports expanded rapidly along with recovery of the world economy, and income from overseas construction increased due to the construction boom in the Middle East. However, the rapid growth of monetary aggregates -- of around 40 percent a year -- resulting especially from the inflow of liquidity from abroad, generated pressure for inflation. Speculative booms, meanwhile, occurred in the markets for real estate, stocks, and commodities in short supply[10]. These factors, i.e., over-heated economy, speculative boom in asset markets, inflation, wage increases, were what weakened the competitiveness of domestic firms in the international export markets.

(2) Duplicated and Excessive Investment in Heavy and Chemical Industries

The adverse effects of the policy of promoting heavy and chemical industries, and of the hasty and aggressive implementation thereof in the late 1970s, included the increases in the number of delinquent firms and distortions in industrial structure. These problems, among others, caused the 1980 economic crisis. Firms which had initially been skeptical of investing in the heavy and chemical industries till the early 1970s, rushed to participate in the investment projects after confirming the government's determination to foster these industries. The amount of investment was too large, however, compared to the sizes of the markets. The capacity utilization of firms investing in new projects was so low that they could not reach the break-even point. Stagnation of the domestic economy and the world

[10] In those days, the prices of real assets rose so sharply that the period was called an "age of premium"; the price of human capital, i.e., wages, also increased rapidly due to a labor shortage (Korea Development Institute 1981, p. 5).

economy alike lowered the profitability of firms further and drove the heavy and chemical industries into a state of potential delinquency. Moreover, concentration of resources on the heavy and chemical industries resulted in short supplies of necessities and other products of light industries, and eroded long-term growth potentials of those industries.

(3) Repressive Economic Policy

The Korean economy in the 1970s was a repressed economy[11], if not a completely planning economy, in the sense that there existed a large amount of government control and intervention in the operation of the economic system. Since the August 3rd Decree in 1972, the government controlled commodity prices, interest rates, and exchange rates and continually intensified its intervention in resource allocation.

Seen from a structural point of view, the crisis beginning in 1979 was a result of the vulnerability stemming from the structural weaknesses or inefficiencies of a repressed economy. The policy makers those days also shared this view. The Economic Planning Board, for example, in its Comprehensive Economic Stabilization Policy promulgated on April 17th, 1979, stressed that structural policy measures were in need for fostering the growth potential of Korean economy in the long run (Korea Development Institute 1981, p. 371). In a similar context, the Bank of Korea attributed the then crisis to structural problems (The Bank of Korea, *1980 Annual Report*, p. 1), and asserted that the managerial efficiency and financial structures of firms should be improved to enhance their competitiveness (p. 8).

Repressive policy measures might have been unavoidable in order to foster the nation's infant industries. It is also true, however, that they distorted and weakened the economic structure. For example, interest rate ceilings brought about such problems as excess demand for bank loans, prevalence of the curb money market, and decreased incentives to save. Policy loans and required approval of foreign borrowings led not only to economic problems such as over-borrowings by firms, but also to non-economic problems such as cronyism, i.e., 'intimate' relationships between firms and the government. Direct control by the government stifled the individual will to innovate and thus discouraged the spontaneity essential for a harmonious working of the market system. Due to the intensive government intervention in the financial sector, financial institutions had little incentive to screen loan applicants and monitor borrowers, and also lacked

---

[11] The term "repressed economy" refers to an economy in which the government severely intervenes in private sector's resource allocation via price and quantity controls. For details as to repression, see MacKinnon (1973), Krueger (1993), Fry (1995), and others.

initiative in developing new financial techniques. Firms tended to seek profit maximization not so much through managerial innovation as through lobbying the government. Consequently, it seems highly likely that the government's control weakened the private sector's adaptability to changing economic environment.

The government's control of the economy is also likely to have stalled growth in the sophistication of the economic system and to have made it fragile to external shocks. In order to increase the flexibility of an economy, it is necessary to allow for a variety of heterogeneous elements in the system. Strict control by the government, however, led to an unsophisticated or monotone economic structure, which was more fragile than a sophisticated one.

(4) Imbalances Between Real and Financial Sectors (Underdevelopment of Financial Sector)

From the beginning of its economic development, Korea chose an unbalanced growth strategy for economic development, and pursued it faithfully. This produced various inter-sectoral imbalances, among them imbalances between real and financial sectors, begotten by the policy of promoting industrialization through financial repression. These imbalances became one of the major background factors behind the 1980 economic crisis. The degree of imbalance had intensified all the more because of the August 3rd Decree in 1972, which forced the financial sector to sacrifice for the sake of the real sector, especially the large firms, by means of a compulsive conversion of debt contracts and rescheduling, with a suppression of interest rates to below the market rates. Even though the decree contained some measures to encourage financial development, such as the establishment of non-banking financial institutions, it lacked respect for market principles in development of the financial sector. Behind this lay the developmentalist view that financial development was only supplementary to industrial development. Since the government controlled the commercial banks, investors did not find any incentive to buy bank stocks, and this of course hampered issuance of stocks by the banks[12]. In the late 1970s, there were cases where no single nation-wide commercial bank had even as much capital as the amount needed to finance a large investment project proposal by a big business firm. Among the most harmful effects of these imbalances between the real and financial sectors were retardation of the banks' capabilities to monitor and check firms' activities, and inability of the banks to restrain over-borrowings and inefficient use of them by firms.

---

[12] At that time, the government was the largest stockholder in four out of the five nation-wide commercial banks.

C. Measures to Cope with the 1980 Crisis

The set of economic policies implemented from 1979 to the early 1980s to cope with the economic crisis consisted of a macroeconomic stabilization policy, an export promotion and foreign exchange policy, deregulation, measures to correct inefficient and duplicate investment projects, and others as microeconomic measures.

First, the government implemented a macroeconomic stabilization policy, beginning from 1979 when the domestic economy showed stagnation along with steeply increased international oil prices. The policy was promulgated as the Comprehensive Economic Stabilization Measures on April 17th, 1979. It consisted of measures to stabilize the prices of products and the supply of necessities, fiscal restriction, restructuring of heavy and chemical industries, and increases in the interest rates paid on bank deposits. The basis of the stabilization was maintained relatively consistently thereafter. The only exception was the expansionary monetary policy sought after June 1980 to boost the economy. To counter the destabilizing effects of this monetary expansion, stronger fiscal restriction was pursued. In order to control increases in expenditures, the government adopted a zero-base budget formula from 1981 on. In line with macroeconomic measures, stabilization was pursued through direct and microeconomic measures such as release of government-stock rice, strengthening direct controls on prices of major products, and anti-speculation policy in the real estate market.

Second, the government implemented a policy to promote exports and support firms' repayments of foreign debts, to alleviate the burden of foreign debt servicing by firms. The Won was devalued in January 1980. At the same time, the government increased its subsidies to exporting activities by increasing the loan for trade. In order to help public corporations and the heavy and chemical industries repay their foreign debts, the government introduced a special foreign-currency loan program on April 3rd, 1980. It also opened the stock market as part of an economic liberalization program, and tried to induce foreign capital by establishing an investment fund exclusively for foreigners, the first ever vehicle for foreigners' indirect investment in domestic securities.

Third, the government pushed forward a liberalization policy, admitting that the economic difficulties at that time stemmed from structural inefficiencies formed by its own excessive economic intervention. In the financial sector, the government privatized the nation-wide commercial banks, attempted to allow for more autonomy for bank management, and reduced the extent of policy loans. On September 6th, 1979, it introduced a new system for setting interest rates at individual banks, utilizing spreads over prime rate replacing the previous system of government-set interest rate ceilings. Subsequently, the government introduced new financial instruments, whose rates of returns could supposedly be determined by market forces, such as commercial papers (CPs), cash management accounts (CMAs), and negotiable certificates of deposits (CDs). The Bank of Korea tried to shy away from direct control of the domestic credits of financial institutions and introduced an indirect mode of managing the money supply, utilizing the price function of the interest rate from January 7th, 1982. As for industrial policy, the government changed from a selective to a functional or across-the-board intervention mode. In 1986, it abolished the seven acts pertaining to promotion of seven individual industries and enacted the 'Industry Development Act,' which integrated and unified these former acts. The thrust of this move was to provide a means to support industries across-the-board. With this measure, it became possible for preferential loans to be provided to an unspecified number of firms in the way of supporting exports or purchases of domestically produced machines. The government also promoted trade liberalization in a trial attempt to outgrow the protective industrial policy. On behalf of securing the orderly operation of the market system, the Fair Trade Commission was established. In addition, the legal system was improved in such a way as to change the character of regulations from a positive system to a negative system.[13]

Fourth, in response to worsening cash flows and excess capacity in the heavy and chemical industries, the government established measures to restructure these industries. On the basis of the Heavy and Chemical Industry Coordination Plan, drafted in May 1979, the government tried to coordinate business restructuring, so-called industry rationalization, in such industries as electrical generators, diesel engines, automobiles, electronic switchboards, and transformers. It also attempted to resolve excess-capacity problems in the overseas construction and shipping industries. For various reasons including excessive burdens to financial institutions and recession, however, the so-called industry rationalization policies were not fully implemented prior to the mid-1980s. Measures were also taken to make up for the losses sustained by banks, as these losses had resulted, by and large, from government intervention in the financial sector. On several occasions, the Bank of Korea paid interest on banks' reserve deposits held in accounts in the

[13]Positive list system refers to the legal system in which activities allowed are listed. Those not listed are deemed to be not allowed. Negative list system refers to the legal system in which only those activities not allowed are listed and those not listed are deemed to be allowed. Thus, in general, the positive list system is a more strict and regulatory legal system than the negative list system.

BOK. The government also allowed banks to enter into new businesses, such as the credit card business, with a view to improving their profitability.

Finally, the government implemented several measures to discourage speculation in real estate and reckless management of firms. For example, a measure to improve corporate financial soundness was announced in September 1980, which urged sales of land held for non-business purposes, disposal of affiliate firms and strengthening of external audits for joint-stock corporations. To stabilize the prices of real estate, the government also announced a long-term plan for construction of houses. It also expanded home financing for the lower-income classes.

4. THE POST-1989 "GRAVE SITUATION"

A. Unfolding of the Situation

The economic situation during the period from 1989 to 1992 worsened relatively compared to that in the 1986~1988 period, although not so bad as to constitute an actual economic "crisis." Government officials termed it a "totally grave situation" before others subsequently called it a crisis. Immediately after the high-performance in late 1980s, in which all three major macroeconomic targets--rapid growth, current account surplus, and price stability--had been achieved, things turned the other way; growth, the current account, and prices all worsened simultaneously. At this time, government authorities seemed to be at a loss, as changes in domestic and external conditions brought about many new difficulties for them in designing and implementing proper policies. The term 'grave situation' seems to have been used more to indicate the difficulties in policy implementation than to point to the economic difficulties themselves.

The main economic difficulties then can be described as a slowdown of economic growth, widening current account deficits, and inflation. The economy that had shown double digit growth rates during the 1986~1988 period suddenly slowed down in 1989, growing only 6 percent in that year. Owing to the grand government-promoted project of building 2 million houses, along with a rise in consumption, however, the economy recovered to a growth rate of 9 percent during the following period from 1990 to 1991. Meanwhile, the current account reversed to deficit in 1990 and recorded an even bigger deficit in 1991. The reversal from surplus to deficit reflected the loss of international competitiveness of Korean firms and a large increase in imports. Inflation rose because of excess demand resulting from increased expenditures by residents.

Table 7. Trends of Major Economic Indicators around 1989

	1985	1986	1987	1988	1989	1990	1991	1992
Economic growth[1](%)	6.9	12.4	12.0	11.5	6.2	9.2	8.5	5.1
(manufacturing)	7.1	18.3	18.8	13.4	3.7	9.1	8.9	5.1
Consumption	6.3	8.4	8.1	9.7	10.7	10.1	9.3	6.8
Capital formation	4.7	12.0	16.5	13.4	16.9	24.0	11.8	-0.8
Exports	4.5	26.1	21.6	12.5	-3.8	18.4	12.8	11.0
Imports	-0.6	17.8	19.4	12.8	16.3	29.1	11.0	5.1
Current account (100mil.USD)	-8.9	46.2	98.5	141.6	50.5	-21.8	-87.3	-45.3
WPI[2](rate of change, %)	0.5	-2.6	2.7	2.3	1.2	7.2	1.9	1.6
CPI[2](rate of change, %)	3.1	1.4	6.1	7.2	5.0	9.4	9.3	4.5
M2(end of period, rate of change, %)	11.8	16.8	18.8	18.8	18.4	21.2	18.6	18.4
Consolidated budget balance/GDP(%)	-0.9	-0.1	2.3	1.2	0.0	-0.9	-1.9	-0.7

Note: 1) Growth rate of GDP at 1995 prices.
2) Compared with that of previous year.
Source: The Bank of Korea, *Economic Statistics Yearbook*, various issues.
The Ministry of Finance, *Government Finance Statistics of Korea*, various issues.

An unfavorable world economic situation at this time amplified the worries over stagnation. The dollar was weak in the international financial markets, while competition in the domestic and overseas markets had intensified. Domestically, Korea had to open its markets as promised in its liberalization plans[14], and the Won was on an appreciating trend reflecting the current account surpluses. International oil prices also increased substantially due to the Gulf War in 1990.

Despite the need to respond to this deteriorating economic situation, the government confronted many difficulties in doing so, as proper means were not readily available. Along with the political transition from an authoritarian regime to a democratic regime, public demand for wage increases and improvements in the quality of life became uncontrollable, so that the government could not find ways to constrain wages or consumption increases. Direct controls were unthinkable because of the economic liberalization trend. For example, after the government adopted a market average exchange rate system on March 2nd, 1990, its influence on exchange rates diminished to a great extent. Seen from this point

[14] After succeeding in opening the Japanese economy through the *Yen-Dollar Committee* in 1984, the US government pressed Korea for market opening.

of view, the economic crisis at that time was indeed actually more of a policy dilemma in nature, in that the government was unable to offer proper means to deal with the economic difficulties.

B. Background of the Situation

(1) Speculative Boom

Against the economic boom in the latter half of the 1980s, another round of speculative boom appeared in the stock and real estate markets. The stock price index, which had been 137 in October 1985, began to rise from around the end of 1985, and reached 1,003 in March 1989 (refer to Figure 2). This long-rising trend of stock prices was followed by jumps in the prices of land and houses from around 1988. The prices of land and houses increased 129 and 56 percent, respectively, during the period from the end of 1987 to the end of 1991 (refer to Figure 3).

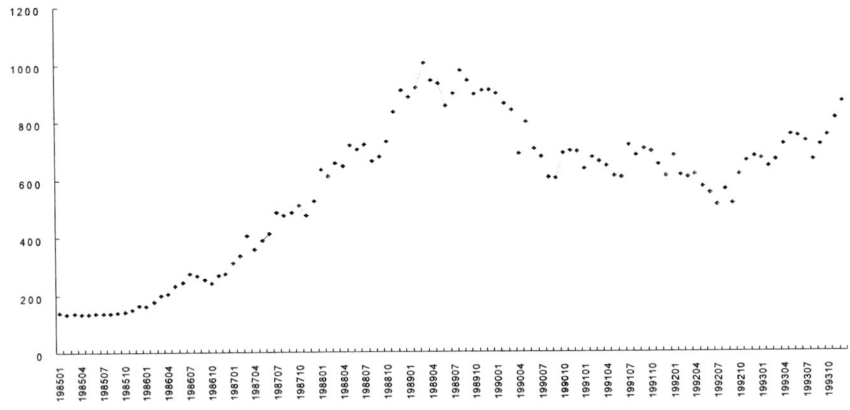

Source: Korea Stock Exchange, *Stock*, various issues.

Figure 2. Trends of Stock Price Index

These asset bubbles caused several disturbances to the economy as they spread, even though there were no cases of their sudden bursting. Speculative demand for credit increased rapidly as speculators financed their investments through bank loans. The resultant increases in interest rates eroded the international competitiveness of domestic firms. Due to the wealth effects of the asset appreciation, consumption and construction investment increased. The changes in the structure of aggregate demand from exports to domestic demand generated worries over erosion of the home base for export production. The proportion of GDP consumed by the private sector or invested in construction was 65.5 percent in 1988, but it increased to 76 percent by the early 1990s. Moreover, the firms sought capital gains from the real assets, while neglecting their needs to improve managerial efficiency, and this weakened their competitive edge even further.

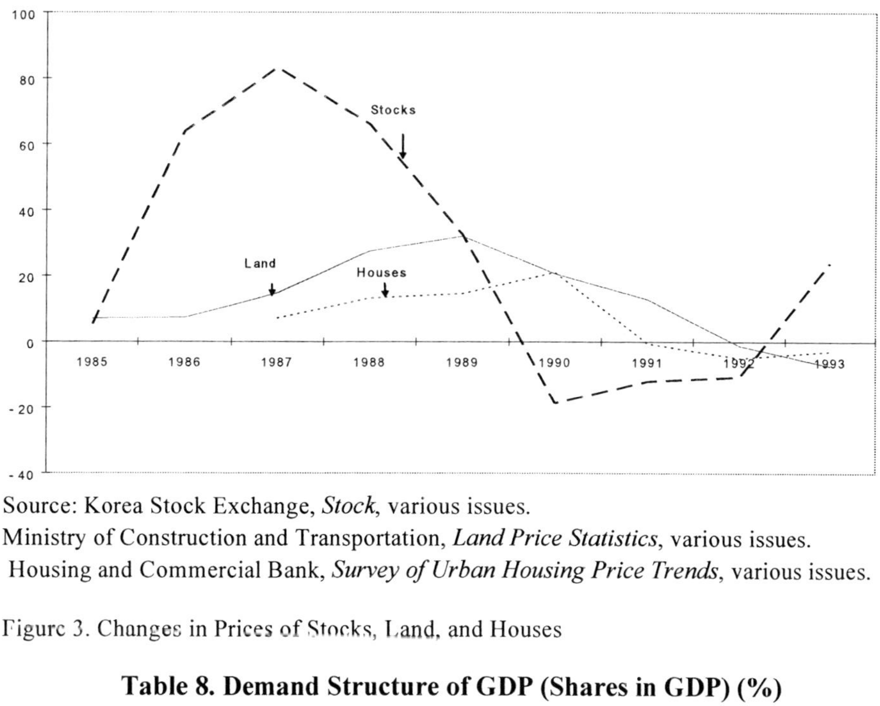

Source: Korea Stock Exchange, *Stock*, various issues.
Ministry of Construction and Transportation, *Land Price Statistics*, various issues.
Housing and Commercial Bank, *Survey of Urban Housing Price Trends*, various issues.

Figure 3. Changes in Prices of Stocks, Land, and Houses

Table 8. Demand Structure of GDP (Shares in GDP) (%)

	1980	1985	1988	1989	1990	1991	1992
Private Consumption(A)	63.4	57.5	50.0	52.0	52.3	52.3	52.9
Construction(B)	18.0	16.2	15.5	17.6	22.2	24.2	23.1
A+B	81.4	73.7	65.5	69.6	74.5	76.5	76.0

Source: The Bank of Korea, *National Account*, various issues.

(2) Liberalization and Democratization Accompanied by Eruption of Demand for Basic Needs

While liberalization had been a basic theme since the early 1980s in the economic sphere, democratization had also progressed steadily in the political sphere. The June 29th Democratization Declaration in 1987 set the stage for a jump in the number of labor disputes. Rapid increases in wages[15], together with social unrest, caused a decline in the international competitiveness of Korean firms and lowered international confidence in the Korean economy. In this situation, an economic opening policy, including freed overseas travel and liberalization of luxury consumer goods imports[16], was also promoted in order to help manage the large current account surplus. Owing to income and wealth growth, and to the appreciation of the Won, these measures triggered increases in consumption, especially of luxuries. This in turn caused workers to ask for further wage increases and led to more labor disputes. The 1988 Olympics held in Seoul also brought about a laxity in social discipline.

(3) Changes in World Economic Environment

The worsening of the world economy and the Won appreciation together aggravated the difficulties of the government in conducting economic policies. By then, international pressure was growing for Korea to increase its role in the international community, commensurate with its improved economic status. Specifically, pressure from advanced countries mounted for the opening of Korean markets. This was a fundamental change in trade policy for these countries, which had previously preferred to stall rapid increases of imports from Korea. Moreover, as the WTO system was expected to come into effect before long, there arose worries about foreign firms' taking over domestic markets in agricultural products and financial services, as well as markets for manufactured goods.

(4) Lessened Effectiveness of Economic Policies

One of the background factors of the post-1989 grave situation was that the old-style economic policies could not respond effectively to the changes brought about by economic liberalization and movements in the domestic and world economic environments. The economic situation was nothing exceptionally

---

[15] It is highly probable that the wage rate would have increased, the democratization decree notwithstanding, since the unemployment rate in late 1980 stayed at the level of 2 percent, well below the projected natural unemployment rate of 3 percent.

severe, but the government nevertheless called the situation a grave one. The reason was that the policy makers felt ill-equipped to handle the situation. In fact, institutions, including an adequately working market mechanism, had not evolved sufficiently to incorporate the new economic order required under the liberalized system. The government had lost the use of its previous policy instruments and had not yet developed the capabilities needed to coordinate economic matters under drastically changed economic conditions.

In addition, it was hardly possible to come up with a solution to disentangle the combination of stagnant stock markets and over-heated real estate markets. An expansionary macroeconomic policy would help support stock prices, but it would hamper the efforts to stabilize real estate prices.

C. Measures to Cope with the Situation

The economic policies in this period comprised an industrial restructuring policy, a measure to stifle real estate speculation, and a policy to boost stock prices. A stabilization policy was also promoted, although not in the sense of managing macroeconomic demand, but rather in the sense of wage stabilizing, stock price stabilization, and asset prices stabilization, control of commodity prices, and stabilization of the living conditions of the common people. From the latter half of 1991, a traditional macroeconomic stabilization policy was pursued. Liberalization and opening were also among the main themes of the policy. During this period, the speed of promotion of liberalization went up.

The industrial restructuring policy aimed at addressing the issue of improving firms' profitability and competitiveness, which had deteriorated due to increasing wages, the Won appreciation, and inflation. As for the mode of policy implementation, the government advocated an indirect provision of support to firms; that is, it tried to remain basically a promoter of infrastructure, basic technology development, and an elastic supply of skilled labor, excepting that it might use direct measures to support the small and medium-sized firms. Despite the government's assertion, however, things were not done so differently from before, as the government provided support to targeted activities directly and frequently twisted the arms of banks to get them to supply the required funds for the preferred sectors. For example, to help firms invest in improving their equipment, the government created special equipment funds on November 14th,

[16] After travel abroad by elderly people was liberalized in January 1988, the policy was applied to all citizens. In addition, import of luxurious home electronic products, such as large refrigerators

1989 and April 4th, 1990, providing loans for this purpose on preferential terms. It also allowed a temporary investment tax deduction on July 4th, 1989, and requested that banks lend in foreign currency to firms which imported new equipment. The government also increased subsidies for exporting activities by increasing the Bank of Korea rediscount proportions applied to foreign trade bills. It also lowered interest rates. In addition, it promoted a policy inducing big business firms to specialize in their core business areas. In order to facilitate this policy, the credit control system was also modified.

One of the priority policy agenda items during this time was cooling the rampant real estate boom. This is well demonstrated by the fact that, during the three years from early 1989 to early 1992, almost twenty related policy measures were announced. This high level of concern was based on the government's judgment that an excessive boom in real estate markets would cause inefficient allocation of resources, trigger demands for wage increases, induce over-consumption, and bring about a sense of incongruity in society by destabilizing the lives of the common people. Thus, the government introduced four laws based on the concept of public ownership of land on December 30th, 1989, and this was meant above all to calm the real estate market[17]. In addition to this, regulations concerning the general land tax (June 16th, 1989), permission for land transactions (December 20th, 1989), and compulsory registration of real estate (April 13th, 1990) were introduced. A measure to encourage the sale of real estate held by big business firms and financial institutions, and one to prevent new acquisition were also introduced. Finally, there was the plan for construction of two million houses, promulgated on April 27th, 1989 with a view to increasing the supply of houses.

Varied measures to stop the steep decrease in stock prices were implemented as stock prices continued to fall after recording their peak in March 1989. On December 12th, 1989, the government announced a policy measure to boost the stock market, and this was followed by measures to control the volume of the stocks issued and to establish a stock market stabilization fund (September 18th, 1990) and a measure to open the stock market to foreign investors (November 30th, 1991). The government also arranged for commercial banks to provide 2.7 trillion Won to investment trust companies, so that these companies could buy stock in the market. On May 27th, 1992, the Bank of Korea supplied 2.9 trillion Won to the investment trust companies to help improve their profit earnings.

---

and large TVs, was liberalized in 1989.

[17] Included in the laws were the Ceiling on Housing Ownership Act, Restitution of Development Gains Act, Land Excess-Profits Tax, Special Account for Land Management and the Balanced Regional Development Act.

Meanwhile, a series of deregulatory measures was put in place with ever-increasing speed, in accordance with the long-term plan for financial liberalization and market opening. In December 1988, interest rates were fully liberalized. Although this policy soon underwent *de facto* repeal when the government's window guidance on determination of interest rates was resumed in response to the sudden economic recession in 1989, it reverted again to plan, when the first stage of the four-stage interest rate liberalization plan of August 1991 was implemented in November 1991. Capital market opening was only partly promoted until 1993, in the form of an increase in the amount of investment funds available exclusively for foreign investors. Then, however, the government announced a comprehensive blueprint for Korea's financial deregulation and capital market opening over the following five years.

Macroeconomic policy in those days was used so as to to boost economic activities, rather than as a tool to stabilize them. As for monetary policy, relatively tight money had been pursued through the introduction and operation of the so-called marginal reserve system until the first half of 1989, as a way of handling the large balance of payments surplus. From the second half of 1989, however, money began to be supplied to fuel an expansionary phase. The reason for this turn-around in monetary policy was a change in the basic goals of monetary policy to include that of providing sufficient funds to the private sector to activate corporate investment and stimulate the stock market. As the economy entered an over-heated phase under the influence of this expansionary policy from 1990 to 1991, the policy took a turn to contraction from the end of 1991. It turned around to expansion once again, however, when the New Economy 5-Year Plan was implemented in 1993.

5. The 1997 Economic Crisis

A. Details of the Crisis

The 1997 economic crisis took place through a complex process: beginning from recession and terms of trade deterioration, then moving to corporate bankruptcies, to banking crises, to contagion from foreign currency crises of South East Asian countries, and to a currency crisis. In addition, during the crisis resolution, a series of corporate bankruptcy and subsequent banking crises repeated itself. The 1997 crisis provided a window for looking at the problems innate in the Korean economic system. This is one of its distinct features.

Table 9. Trends of Inventories (in 1995 constant prices) (Billion Won, %)

	1990	1991	1992	1993	1994	1995	1996	1997	1998
Changes in Inventories	234.2	1,943.6	1,690.1	-1,767.5	2,170.9	1,825.7	3,914.4	-4,218.3	-27,983.1
(Ratios to GDP)	(0.1)	(0.7)	(0.6)	(-0.6)	(0.6)	(0.5)	(1.0)	(-1.0)	(-7.0)

Source: The Bank of Korea, "Recent Trends of Inventories," *Press Release* 2000-1-17.

Before going into the details of the 1997 crisis, this book first takes a look at the economic situation in 1996. Above all, it should be noted that the economy slowed down in 1996, after showing a high growth rate of over 8 percent a year on average in 1994 and 1995. At a first glance, the 1996 slowdown looked like a soft landing, since GDP grew almost 5 percent that year.

Looking at the details of economic growth in 1996, however, one can find problems in the Korean economy. The nearly 5% growth rate was mainly attributable to increases in inventories, which occurred as firms struggled to continue production under sluggish demand. The reason for this was that the cost of stopping factory operation was extremely high in processing industries such as the petrochemical, steel, and semiconductors, which are the major industries in the Korean economy. The volume of inventories began to weigh heavily on the corporate sector. The portion of inventory increases in GDP mounted up to 1 percent. Thus, if it had not been for the increase in inventories, the economic growth rate in 1996 would have ended up at the mere 3 percent level.

The current account deficit, which had been increasing from 1994 to 1995, amounted to 23 billion dollars, 5 percent of GDP in 1996. Decreases in the prices of major exports, such as semiconductors, and continuous increases in imports were main contributory factors to the widening deficit of the current account. Moreover, the decrease in the unit prices of exports, combined with increases in export volume, worsened the profitability of exporting activities.

Table 10. Decomposition of Exports

	Amount of Exports [1]	Amount Index [2]	Unit Value Index [2]	Volume Index [2]
1990	650.2	52.0	94.2	55.2
1991	718.7	57.5	94.7	60.7
1992	766.3	61.3	93.2	65.9
1993	822.4	65.7	93.6	70.2
1994	960.1	76.7	95.2	80.7
1995	1,250.6	100.0	100.0	100.0
1996	1,297.2	103.7	86.6	119.8
1997	1,361.6	108.9	72.8	149.6
1998	1,323.1	105.8	60.5	174.9

Note: 1) In 100 million US dollars

2) Indices express values relative to 100 in 1995.

Source: The Bank of Korea, *Economic Statistics Yearbook*, various issues.

Table 11. Trends of Major Economic Indicators Around 1997

	1993	19 94	1995	1996	1997	1998
Economic growth[1)](%)	5.7	8.4	8.2	4.8	2.4	-7.1
(manufacturing)	5.4	10.8	11.3	6.8	6.6	-7.2
Consumption	5.4	7.1	8.2	7.2	3.2	-8.2
Capital formation	6.3	10.7	11.9	7.3	-2.2	-21.1
Exports	11.3	16.1	24.6	11.2	21.4	13.3
Imports	6.2	21.6	22.4	14.2	3.2	-22.0
Current account (100mil.USD)	9.9	-38.7	-85.1	-230.0	-81.7	403.6
WPI(rate of change, %)	1.5	2.7	4.7	3.2	3.9	12.2
CPI(rate of change, %)	4.8	6.2	4.5	4.9	7.5	0.8
M_2(end of period, rate of change, %)	18.6	15.6	15.5	16.2	19.2	19.0
Budget balance[2)]/GDP(%)	0.08	0.53	0.45	0.03	-0.02	-2.97

Note: 1) Growth rate of GDP at 1995 prices

2) On the basis of the central government budget

Source: The Bank of Korea, *Economic Statistics Yearbook,* various issues.

Table 12. Trends of Foreign Debt (end of period, 100 mil. dollars)

	1992	1993	1994	1995	1996	1997	
						11p	12p
<IMF criterion>							
Long-term	260 (..) <41.2>	267 (2.9) <39.9>	303 (13.5) <34.2>	410 (35.5) <34.2>	575 (40.3) <36.5>	729 (26.7) <45.0>	860 (49.5) <55.7>
Short-term	370 (..) <58.8>	403 (8.9) <60.1>	584 (44.9) <65.8>	787 (34.9) <65.8>	1,000 (27.1) <63.5>	889 (-11.1) <55.0>	685 (-31.6) <44.3>
Total Foreign Debt	629 (..)	670 (6.4)	887 (32.4)	1,197 (35.0)	1,575 (31.6)	1,618 (2.7)	1,544 (-2.0)
<World Bank criterion>							
Total Foreign Debt	428	439	568	784	1,047	1,161	1,208
Long-term	243	247	265	331	437	545	696
Short-term	185	192	304	453	610	616	512

Notes: 1) Numbers in ( ) denote rates of change and those in < > denote composition ratios.

Source: The Bank of Korea, *Statistical Yearbook of Foreign Exchange,* 1998.

The total foreign debt of residents was climbing rapidly at that time, increasing from 120 billion U.S. dollars at the end of 1995 to 160 billion U.S. dollars at the end of 1996. This was mainly attributable to the widening current account deficit, but it was also influenced by increases in foreign borrowings by domestic firms and financial institutions following capital account liberalization.

Because of a recession with increased financial burdens of firms, entering 1997, cases of corporate insolvency began to propagate, and the banking sector's non-performing loans accumulated accordingly. Starting with the Hanbo Steel Company, which went bankrupt on January 23rd, 1997, the *chaebols* (Korean big business groups) began going under in a series consisting of Sammi, Jinro, Daenong, Hanshin-Gongyoung, and others. Accordingly, the portion of non-performing loans (classified as substandard, doubtful, and estimated loss credits) in total loans of banks rose from 4.1 percent at the end of 1996 to 6.0 percent at the end of 1997. These bankruptcies of big business groups revealed the evils of the Korean economy implied by cronyism or cozy relationships between political groups and businesses, and played a crucial role in the loss of Korea's economic credibility in the international community.

Under these circumstances, then, the Thailand Baht suddenly plummeted on July 2nd, 1997, signaling the beginning of currency crises in South East Asian countries. The Baht had been put under speculative attack as the Thai government attempted to maintain its value, while at the same time bailing out the troubled financial institutions in the wake of a bubble-like boom and bust, and collapse in the real estate market. Through contagion effects, the currencies of Malaysia, Indonesia and the Philippines, which were in similar situations or had close trade relationships with Thailand, also began steep depreciation. Afterwards, the speculative attacks on currencies spread to Taiwan and Hong Kong.

Immediately after the South East Asian currency crises, Kia Motors became insolvent, and foreign investors' confidence in the Korean economy was further undermined by the protracted resolution of the Kia Motors' problem. After the speculative attacks on the Taiwan and Hong Kong currencies took place, international credit rating agencies downgraded Korea's sovereign credit rating. From then on, international financial institutions would hardly agree to roll over their loans to Korean financial institutions. Korea's domestic financial institutions, no longer able to obtain finance abroad, were forced to purchase foreign currency on the domestic foreign exchange market for their daily settlements. The Bank of Korea accordingly provided them with foreign reserves, and the nation's stock of foreign reserves was rapidly depleted as the financial institutions failed to recover their credit-worthiness. In consequence, the Korean government asked the International Monetary Fund for emergency credits.

Immediately after the announcement of the IMF stand-by credit agreements and the associated IMF/IBRD economic reform program, the economic situation in Korea became genuinely critical due to break-down of financial intermediaries under the widening spread of business bankruptcies, to the point where normal operation of the economy was seriously threatened. Shortly thereafter, however, credits from international financial agencies flowed in, foreign debts began to be rolled over, and the balance of payments turned to surplus. In addition, the crisis began to be resolved, as Korean firms and financial institutions showed progress in restructuring. With these developments, the foreign exchange markets began to calm down, and Korea was able to emerge from the crisis situation.

The above discussions indicate that the 1997 economic crisis comprised a number of different characteristics -- a corporate crisis, a banking (financial) crisis, a currency crisis, and a policy-driven crisis. It was nevertheless the typical type of economic crisis defined in Chapter 2, since the whole economic system was close to collapse.

B. Background of the 1997 Crisis

Since the nature of the 1997 crisis was so complicated, its causes may not be summarized by only one or two factors[1]. But for the sake of comparison with the other crises that happened in Korea, the following may be enumerated as important factors of the 1997 crisis:

(1) Over-investment

It is doubtful that the economy had been in an over-heated state in the period from 1994 to 1995, or that a speculative boom had occurred. The economic growth rates during the period were not as high as those in the past boom periods; investment showed no more than a mild increase. Thus, the economy at the time can hardly be viewed as having been in an over-heated state, let alone a speculative boom.

From the viewpoint of industrial organization, however, the problem lay in the excessive-competition and over-investment in major industries, which resulted when many of the big business groups expanded their business areas by entering industries already full of competition. Heterogeneous business conglomeration, a type of business integration of companies whose products were largely unrelated

[1] In light of this, discussions in the Korean media after late November, when the currency crisis began to emerge, attributed the crisis to political, social, and cultural factors as well as economic ones.

to each other, increased rapidly from the mid-1990s. During this period, the firms seemed to have actively diversified their business areas in response to the trend toward globalization and domestic market opening. However, their strategy of entering new industries was ill-founded; the big business firms were seldom observed entering new and promising industries based on their own technological innovation. Rather, most of them entered industries in which other firms had already become established, and were known to be realizing high profit rates. The *chaebols* competed with each other in building petrochemical, electronic, and automobile factories, facilities for the distribution industry, and in the construction business. Such competition led to over- and duplicated capacity. Table 13 shows that heterogeneous business conglomeration, compared to other types of corporate integration, increased rapidly from the mid-1990s. Such over-investment resulted in over-production, and the profit prospects of the firms involved became dim. This over-investment underlined the inefficiency of the Korean economic system as a whole, and from time to time, triggered worries over the solvency of these firms.

Table 13. Cases of Corporate Integration

	1991	1992	1993	1994	1995	1996	1997
Horizontal integration	43	39	36	40	58	73	78
Vertical integration	45	38	34	24	43	69	80
Conglomeration	66	72	53	131	224	252	260

Note: Horizontal integration brings together similar or related business types. Vertical integration occurs between businesses that have a supplier-customer relationship. A conglomeration integrates firms whose products are largely unrelated to each other with each other.

Source: Korea Fair Trade Commission, *White Book of Fair Trade*, various issues.

(2) Over-borrowings and Maturity Mismatches

Deterioration in the financial structures of firms from the mid-1990s was one of the important factors behind the 1997 economic crisis. While firms expanded into new business areas, the economy began to stagnate, and corporate cash flows dried up. The firms thus attempted to meet their increased needs for funds through external financing. This practice was especially notable from 1996, when the economy entered a recession period. The debt-equity ratio in Korean manufacturing was 396 percent at the end of 1997[2], which was 110 percent points higher than that at the end of 1995.

In the midst of globalization and capital account liberalization, corporations placed securities in the international financial markets on the strength of their own credits and increased their short-term borrowings of trade credits. Table 15 shows a big increase in the non-bank private sector's foreign borrowings.

Table 14 . Financial Indicators of Manufacturing in the 1990s (%)

	1990	91	92	93	94	95	96	97
Debt-equity ratio	282.5	306.7	318.7	294.9	302.5	286.8	317.1	396.3
Financial expenses-sales Ratio	5.12	5.69	6.31	5.93	5.64	5.57	5.84	6.39
Net income-total assets Ratio	1.48	1.41	0.89	1.04	1.90	2.83	0.50	-0.93
Current ratio	99.44	95.33	92.75	94.13	95.59	95.39	91.89	91.76

Source: The Bank of Korea, *Financial Statement Analysis*, various issues.

Table 15. Foreign Debt by Borrowers (end of period, 100 mil. US dollars)

	1992	93	94	95	96	97
Public Sector	56 <8.9>	38 <5.7>	36 <4.0>	30 <2.5>	24 <1.5>	180 <11.7>
Non-Bank Private Sector	137 <21.8>	156 <23.4>	200 <22.6>	261 <21.8>	356 <22.6>	423 <27.4>
Financial Sector	436 <69.3>	475 <70.9>	651 <73.4>	905 <75.6>	1,195 <75.9>	941 <60.9>
Total Foreign Debts	629	670	887	1,197	1,575	1,544

Notes: 1) Numbers in < > denote composition ratio (%).
Source: The Bank of Korea, *Statistical Yearbook of Foreign Exchange*, 1998.

Excessive maturity mismatches of debts were among the main factors that caused the 1997 economic crisis. Firms suffered from liquidity problem because

[2] The sharp rise in the debt-equity ratios of firms in 1997 was due partly to the steep depreciation of the Korean Won. But the Financial Statement Analysis of the Bank of Korea shows that the amount of debts denominated in foreign currencies owed by the manufacturing firms was about 10 trillion Won, which was not more than 3 percent of total debts. Even without the depreciation in 1997, the debt-equity ratio would have reached the level of 370~ 380 percent, considering that the loss from foreign exchange revaluation amounted to about 9 trillion Won and the capital stock was about 102 trillion Won.

their investments had not yielded normal profits yet, while a lot of their funds were fixed due to investments. For Korean manufacturing industry, the current ratio, i.e., the ratio of liquidity assets to liquidity liability, was a mere 92 percent at the end of 1996, the lowest recorded during the 1990s[3].

The same problems of the maturity mismatches occurred in the external sector as well. Firms and banks came to rely more and more on short-term foreign debt during this period. The ratio of short-term to total foreign debt at the end of 1996 was 63.5 percent by the IMF criterion, and 58.3 percent by the World Bank criterion as shown in Table 12. The short-term debt increased because current account deficits were financed mainly through short-term borrowings by financial institutions and through trade credits by business firms. The financial institutions used too much of the foreign exchange funds that they financed on short-term bases to make long-term investments. Moreover, the domestic financial institutions' investments were concentrated in the markets of the South East Asian countries and Russia, which went sour when those countries experienced currency crises at almost the same time as Korea did. Meanwhile, official foreign reserves were allocated in such a way that sufficient reserves could not be secured. Fairly large amount of Korea's foreign reserves were deposited with domestic banks and their overseas branches, and deposits could not be withdrawn in an emergency.

(3) Lack of Discipline

The lack of market discipline was another factor behind the 1997 crisis. Market discipline was at very disappointing level. Even though the country had already undergone such big changes as political democratization, economic liberalization, and market opening, Since government control or management had been able to deter economic agents from engaging in hazardous activities, the past government-led development system had at least been capable of sustaining itself, even if it could not attain the first best efficiency. With the results of economic liberalization and market opening, however, the government had been largely removed from such a role. Nevertheless, a new market discipline, the so-called market mechanism, had not been settled down.

Even after financial liberalization, for example, financial institutions remained too inactive to take on the role of checking and monitoring the behavior of customer firms. Nor were stockholders so active in monitoring managers as might have been expected, in light of the increased importance of the capital markets as the channel of financial resource allocation. Disclosure of information

---

[3] The current ratio decreased further to the level of below 90 percent in 1998 when corporate insolvencies increased steeply.

essential for checking management performance was also insufficient, while the role of credit evaluation agencies had not been established, either.

Regulation and supervision of financial institutions were still hardly developed. Prudential regulation was known to be essential in a liberalized environment, and some regulations had been established. In practice, however, they were neither sufficient nor effectively enforced. In fact, the playing field in the financial sector was tilted in favor of the non-bank financial institutions, leaving them with regulatory loopholes or loose supervision. Some of them, while lacking adequate capabilities to manage risk, nevertheless took extremely high risks in pursuit of high returns.

Failure to form a new disciplinary mechanism led to a situation in which individual actors' optimal choices conflicted with those of others or deviated from the social optimum. Making matters worse was the fact that there were no longer corrective actions which could be effectively taken. The government tendencies to gloss over the economic situation and practice excessive forbearance were never effectively corrected. Financial institutions took advantage of the implicit public guarantee of deposits, and engaged in gathering as much deposits as possible, while neglecting improvement of their profitability, or their capabilities to manage risk. Firms abused their increased ability to borrow, and engaged in high risk-high return strategies. The owner-managers of *chaebols* maximized their leverage and control, despite their small percentage shares of equity, by abusing mutual debt payment guarantees and cross-share holding. These owner-managers tended to manage a number of large firms dogmatically, or even despotically.

Such problems had been concealed by the brilliant growth performance of the Korean economy. Once revealed, however, they exposed Korean markets to sudden swings in investor confidence, i.e., to a crisis. The foreign -- especially, short-term banking -- capital that had previously flowed in, taking advantage of capital account liberalization and domestic market opening, abruptly withdrew from the Korean markets after confirming that the market's inefficiency stemmed from lack of discipline.

The lack of market discipline was certainly related to the continually accelerating promotion of liberalization before the crisis. One cannot say, however, that liberalization was the direct and fundamental cause for the absence of discipline. Even after liberalization, it takes time and effort -- not only of the government but also of the market participants -- to form market discipline. Thus, it is more to the point to say that a continuation of government control -- different in form but similar in kind to that under the past authoritarian system -- most impeded the formation of market discipline. To say it in another way, the liberalization was led by the government, and in the presence of government control or intervention in the financial sector, private sector initiative was not sufficiently exercised, especially in monitoring and checking the behavior of trade partners.

In this sense, it can be said that the predominance of government influence in the working of the financial sector was a cause for the sector's lack of discipline. The analysis here will not pursue this line any further, however, because termination of the so-called repression would not have automatically brought about market discipline. What is emphasized here is that lack of discipline and the resultant coordination failure exacerbated the adverse effects of the bounded rationality of economic actors, and thus provided a ground for the crisis.

(4) Loss of Confidence in Government's Policy

In some sense, inconsistency and ambiguity in the government's handling of the 1997 crisis exacerbated it. Proper action taken by the government in accordance with the circumstances would have prevented a critical situation from proceeding to a crisis or collapse. This had, in fact, always been the case in the past, when critical situations arose due to the government's pursuit of too rapid economic growth; through successful adaptations to the situations at such times, the government had always been able to preserve market confidence. In 1997, however, the government's policy response was unable to generate market participants' confidence. The government could not find its proper role in a market economy system. It failed to correctly diagnose the economic fundamentals, and to design the right prescription to cure what ailed them. It sometimes hid policy information that would have served the economy better if disclosed. It struggled to resist market forces even when it was obvious that accepting them was a better option. It failed to stop the propagation of the crisis; it did not heed the lessons of past experience, even after it had seen a few rounds of the crisis propagation process: corporate insolvencies leading to banking distress, and then to the near depletion of foreign reserves. In retrospect, there were several chances for the government to break the Korean economy's rolling in the vicious circle leading towards economic crisis in 1997. In this respect, the Korean government's policy mistakes during the years 1996 and 1997 can be listed as one of the factors behind the 1997 economic crisis

C. Policy Response

The government took varied measures to cope with the 1997 economic crisis, based on the recognition that the crisis resulted from accumulated structural imbalances in many areas. The main framework for crisis resolution, which was molded after the method of general IMF crisis resolution, was stated in the stand-by agreement, or letter of intent. It was composed of a macroeconomic stabilization policy and a microeconomic structural adjustment policy. The former was centered on restriction of domestic demand and expenditure-switching, to correct the balance of payments deficits. Exchange rates were thus allowed to depreciate freely and reflect market forces fully. At the same time, money market rates were raised sharply to control the inflationary impact of the Won depreciation. This extremely tight macroeconomic policy aimed at both restraining domestic expenditures and preventing capital outflows. The microeconomic structural adjustment policy, meanwhile, included measures to resolve structural problems in each market. Its fundamental theme was to establish the institutional setting for a well-functioning market mechanism.

Under the above framework, implementation of policies was practiced on the basis of a moving target approach, in which specific policy targets were changed according to circumstances. Right after the currency crisis, the primary target was to calm the foreign exchange markets through a sharp hike of money market rates, and to restore investors' confidence in the Korean economy through announcement of a restructuring plan, including the exit of troubled banks and the restructuring of industrial investments. From May 1998, when the foreign exchange market began to calm down and the Won stabilized, monetary policy was relaxed and the money market rates were lowered, in consideration of the by-then increased uncertainty in the domestic financial markets. The instability of domestic financial markets in mid-1998 reflected the credit crunch and wide-spread bankruptcy of firms at that time. The credit crunch resulted because all banks undergoing screening by the supervising authority, for possible market exits, refrained from lending. The widespread number of bankruptcy was due partly to this and partly to the high level of interest rates.

Table 16. IMF Reform Program

	Sector	Contents
Macro-Economic Policy	monetary and exchange rate policy	• tight money to contain inflation and limit downward pressure on the Won – large liquidity injection to be reversed, and money market rates raised – day-to-day conduct of monetary policy to be guided by movements in the exchange rates and short-term interest rates – targeting growth of M_3, reserve money, and net domestic assets of the BOK
	fiscal policy	• tightened to achieve a surplus – raising transportation tax, special excise tax, broadening the tax base – reducing current expenditures
Micro-economic Structural Adjustment Policy	financial sector	• comprehensive restructuring and strengthening of the financial system to make it sound, transparent, and more efficient – a clear and firm exit policy, strong market and supervisory discipline, increased competition
	trade and capital account liberalization	• streamlined import certification procedure and other trade-related regulations • acceleration of ongoing capital account liberalization program
	corporate governance and corporate financial structure	• improvement of corporate governance through financial reform and capital liberalization – easing restrictions on M&As, introduction of internationally accepted practices in accounting and consolidated balance sheets, revision of bankruptcy provisions, break from past policies of bail-outs
	labor market	• easing dismissal restrictions to improve labor market flexibility – facilitation of reemployment to ease the burden of layoffs

Source: IMF (1997).

Structural adjustment was largely divided into two stages. The first stage involved establishing basic institutions needed for smooth operation of a market economic system, and forcing insolvent firms and banks out of the market. For this purpose, varied policy measures were undertaken. The institutional capabilities for restructuring were enhanced by integrating the three extant financial supervisory agencies into one agency, the Financial Supervision Commission, and by expanding the function of Korea Deposit Insurance Corporation (KDIC), and establishing Korea Asset Management Corporation (KAMCO) to dispose of non-performing loans. Bankruptcy law provisions were amended and M&A restrictions eased. Disclosure requirements for accounting information were also strengthened, and measures to improve corporate governance introduced, to provide for better monitoring and supervision of corporate or bank managers by interested parties. The authorities also devised measures to restrain over-borrowing by firms, such as prohibition of mutual debt guarantees among firms in the same large business groups. The government forced extremely troubled banks to exit the market, and at the same time used public funds to buy non-performing loans from and recapitalize the viable ones. It let the main creditor banks lead the debt workout programs to liquidate delinquent firms.

The second stage structural adjustment plan aimed at improving the management and governance of firms and banks through their own initiatives. So far, however, firms and banks were not ready to enter this stage. This is mainly because the amounts of non-performing loans increased to an unexpectedly large extent, and because the first stage restructuring was delayed due to unexpected events such as the Daewoo Group's going into a workout program.

Chapter 3

APPRAISAL OF POLICIES FOR RESOLVING THE CRISES IN THE PAST

1. THE 1972 CRISIS

The policies incorporated in the August 3rd Decree were evaluated by the authority as a success (The Bank of Korea 1973). The appraisal was based on economic performance, such as visible improvement in corporate financial structures and expansion of exports one year or so after the policies were implemented.

Seen from the present point of view, however, it can be said that the Decree was problematic in some ways; also, its effects were not so great in the long run. The nature of the economic crisis had been rightly identified as a corporate crisis, and the focus of policy appropriately put on improving the financial structure of firms and modernizing the financial system by introducing non-bank financial institutions. The problem lay in the methods used in pursuit of this policy. Especially, the write-offs of debts were obviously biased in favor of enterprises and against finance. The curb loan freeze and rescheduling did not leave room for autonomous financial transactions. It also violated the principle of private ownership and freedom of contracts. The root problem of worsening financial structure of corporations had been their strategies for unsustainably rapid expansion, despite their lack of internal funds. What was actually necessary to improve corporations' financial situations, therefore, was to slow down economic growth and restrain corporations from over-borrowing. Direct subsidies to firms, however, impeded the formation of a reasonable incentive mechanism, and deepened firms' prevalent tendencies to rely on external funds and government support.

The policy of fostering the establishment of non-bank financial institutions served to broaden the scope of the Korean financial system. However, the policy was ineffective in eradicating the curb market, which flourished again in the latter half of the 1970s and first half of the 1980s. Regulatory discrimination between banks and the newly established non-bank financial institutions brought about adverse side effects. The authority gave preferential treatment to the non-bank financial institutions, compared to the banks, in order to help these institutions grow out of their infancy. In this circumstance, the banks lost their market shares, which impeded their sound development. The fragility or weakness of the Korean financial system, a background factor of the 1997 economic crisis, seems to have originated from these policies in the 1970s.

At the time of the 1972 Crisis, the stabilization policy tended to rely on direct controls, rather than on orthodox macroeconomic tools. The government attempted to calm inflation by directly controlling the prices of products such as rice, construction materials, and living necessities. It managed the money supply through direct control of domestic credits from 1970. Unfortunately, this mode of policy implementation brought about adverse side effects afterwards, such as the spread of underground markets and dual prices, and supply shortages of important necessities. In particular, the direct control of domestic credits failed to prevent an excess supply of money in the late 1970s. It eroded the basis of the autonomous operations of banks as well. With regard to the basic stance of macroeconomic policy, in fact, it was expansionary. This was in some sense unavoidable, of course, as stimulating investment in the heavy and chemical industries was given a higher priority than resolving the problems associated with the over-heated economy in the late 1960s. However, the expansionary macroeconomic policy eventually caused over-heating and real estate speculation to spread widely in the late 1970s, and this was among the factors underlying the 1980 economic crisis.

Most of the 1972 crisis resolution measures shared characteristics of direct intervention and subsidies by government. For example, in relieving firms from financial distress, the government intervened directly by freezing their liabilities at the expense of breakdown of the curb market. Thus, the firms enjoyed a free lunch. In short, the crisis resolution measures in the early 1970s were effective to some extent in the short run, but in the long run deepened the structural anomalies of the Korean economy. These structural anomalies paved the way for both the 1980 crisis and the 1997 crisis.

2. THE 1980 CRISIS

The crisis resolution measures for the 1980 economic crisis contained a systematic blueprint based on a synthetic analysis of the various kinds of problems in the Korean economy. The government had at hand a stabilization plan prepared in 1979. The plan generally indicated the right direction for reforming the Korean economy, which was maintained even after the 1980s. Prices were visibly stabilized from 1982, and this contributed to the sustained surpluses in the current account in the latter half of the 1980s. Moreover, the liberalization policy after the crisis was quite consistently and gradually executed. Thus, it put in place a stepping stone for more aggressive liberalization policies in the 1990s.

The crisis resolution measures also laid the groundwork for financial development, both in quantity and in quality. Thanks to price stability, demand for financial assets increased, and correspondingly many new financial instruments were introduced. Especially, the stock and insurance markets, so underdeveloped previously, were able to grow substantially from the mid-1980s when inflation almost ceased. These developments in the financial sector in part reflected shift in emphasis in government's economic policy, from real to financial development, or its recognition of importance of both of them.

The public's perception of economic policy matters also changed as a result of the policy measures introduced in the early 1980s. In particular, the government campaign to deepen public understanding of stabilization policies succeeded, to some extent, in making the public to realize the importance of economic stability, among other objectives, and to accept the shift in policy focus from growth to stability. It seems that these consolidated efforts of the government and the public were rewarded by the country's excellent economic performance later.

Seen from the present point of view, however, the policy measures implemented following the 1980 economic crisis contained some problems as well. The trade-off between growth and stability was neglected, and both were pursued simultaneously. The policy tools for both were mixed together, causing considerable confusion. For example, in the latter half of 1980, about one year after implementation of the stabilization policy, expansionary monetary policy tools were used again. Once again, in the latter half of 1982, the government attempted, (through what were called the June 28th Measures) to activate the economy with a low interest rate policy similar to those in the 1970s. At the same time, the government sought economic stability through tight fiscal policy and direct control of prices. This combination of tight fiscal policy and expansionary monetary policy might be seen as an appropriate policy mix, in that the heavy and chemical industrialization plan required continuous investments by companies lacking internal funds. The fact that from the outset monetary contraction had been ruled out as a means of maintaining economic stability, however, implied that the policy means actually employed might not have been optimally suited to accomplish the policy goals. The fact that monetary policy tools remained only as a means for boosting the economy also indicates that the attitudes of the policy makers had not changed much; that is, they still put great importance to industrial development than to financial development.

The measures taken for liberalization also contained certain problematic aspects. It was then understood that liberalization was inevitable and necessary since the only way to cure the structural problems caused by repression or excessive government control was to liberalize. However, the actual liberalization measures included mostly deregulation of price controls, without serious consideration of need to provide the infrastructure for efficient markets. For example, interest rate liberalization, one of the major targets of liberalization policy, left much to be desired, in terms of stimulating innovation on the part of banks, because it was pursued in a narrow range with various forms of government intervention. It can also be pointed out that liberalization was a government-initiated process, rather than one initiated by private sectors. Thus, it was largely designed to meet the needs of the government, and not those of the private sector. Regarding the speed of the liberalization policy, it put too much importance to a gradual approach to bring about substantial effects. Moreover, it produced adverse side-effects, e.g., institutional disequilibrium such as the uneven playing field between banks and non-bank financial institutions.

In some senses, the nature of many of the economic policies remained largely similar to those in the past, in that such policy tools as controls and intervention were frequently used. Controls were applied to the management of prices, to restraining real estate speculation, and to improving corporate financial structures. In addition, selective industrial policies continued to be pursued through, for example, the Distribution Industry Modernization Plan, the Agricultural Machinery Import-substitution Plan, the Small- and Medium-sized Enterprises Promotion Plan, and the Electronic Industry Promotion Plan.

In short, even though the 1980 crisis resolution policy was rightly directed and performed well in the short run, it had only a limited effect in curing the fundamental problems of the Korean economy. This was verified in part by the similar crises recurred in the 1990s.

3. THE POST-1989 "GRAVE SITUATION"

The government's attempt to overcome a policy-driven crisis by introducing the concept of industrial restructuring seems appropriate. It was also prudent for the government to have maintained consistency in its liberalization policy since the 1980s. There were problems, however. The policy goal was not clearly set, for one thing; and the same policy tools as in the past were applied.

The fact that the target of economic policy was not clear was, in part, due to the lack of a thorough analysis of the causes of the grave situation. The period was in the midst of revolutionary changes in political and social affairs; thus, a radical change in the goals, instruments, and mode of policy implementation was also required. Since the period had seen an eruption of desires that had previously been repressed, showing a stronger tendency for individual actors to pursue their own self-interests, a new policy paradigm, which would accord with these changes, was needed. Economic policy should have addressed such problems as the coordination of conflicting interests and the establishment of market infrastructure, rather than that of managing economic variables to optimal levels. It chose the latter, however; that is, policy makers addressed the short-term issues by making use of direct controls, as in the past. In order to sustain stock prices, for example, the government directly controlled the supply of and demand for stocks. In order to promote industrial restructuring, it provided preferential loans to borrowers importing equipment for factory automation and rationalization, through which many firms were induced to invest in equipment, the same kind pattern as observed in the past.

In another similarity to the past pattern, the government allotted macroeconomic policy to the objective of boosting the economy. Coming as it did after the long economic boom in the late 1980s, the period was characterized by big changes not only in political and social structures, but in consumption patterns as well. To facilitate the economy's adjustment, a dramatic change in policy tone was not desirable at the time, especially because uncertainty needed to be kept to a minimum. Macroeconomic policy, however, was operated in the manner of alternating, within a very short time period, between "stop(contraction)" and "go(expansion)." Furthermore, the economy was then confronted with contradicting trends, such as a slump in stock prices, a rally in real estate price, domestic recession, and a balance of payments deficit. Such a situation hardly yielded itself to a macroeconomic cure. Ideally, macroeconomic policy should have been kept neutral.

The nature of economic policy was not much different from the past, either. As mentioned above, the policy tools included direct controls, and were employed to temporarily address the problems revealed, rather than resolve them fundamentally. Preferential treatment of the real over the financial sector remained unchanged. Some policies were implemented in a manner that contradicted the trend of financial liberalization; for example, the policies for stabilization of stock prices, promotion of investment in manufacturing, and expansion of credits to small- and medium-sized enterprises were backed up mainly by using measures in the financial sector which might repress financial sector development.

In short, the substance of the policy responses to the grave situation in 1989 crisis was to employ direct control measures to resolve the problems which had surfaced. Policy makers neglected probing for a new policy paradigm appropriate for the new socio-economic structure and economic environment. Even worse, these problems innate in the economic system, rather than being fundamentally resolved, were covered over again after the New Economy 5-Year Plan was promoted in 1993.

4. Effectiveness of Crisis Resolutions in the Past

Crises of a similar type have repeatedly taken place under similar backgrounds, such as deterioration of the profitability of firms, over-investment and worsening financial structures, backwardness of the financial sector, and policy mistakes. The genetic processes of all the crises also resembled each other, since they all occurred after economic booms, or in over-heated economies. All in all, the economic crises in Korea may be regarded as having broken out as internal weaknesses -- e.g., over-borrowings by firms -- were exposed to external shocks -- e.g., economic recession, worsening world economic environments, and so on. Similar policy measures were undertaken repeatedly to cope with the crises. In all cases, promotion of investment, through financial and fiscal incentives, was used immediately after the crisis outbreak, and macroeconomic policy was operated on an accommodating base. Moreover, direct controls on prices were frequently employed.

The mere observation that similar crises were being repeated implies that the past crisis resolution policies were not effective. In fact, the past crisis resolution measures consisted mostly of patching over the problems revealed, rather than addressing the root causes of the crises or trying to prevent crises beforehand. Instead, such measures tended more to deepen the structural problems. For example, most of the past crisis resolution measures focused on disposing of the losses incurred by firms and banks through such instruments as bail-outs. This might have lessened the difficulties facing firms and banks at those times; the effects were only temporary, however, and not of such kind as to help improve efficiency. Measures such as subsidies spoiled economic agents' independence and autonomy, eventually allowing them to stick to high leverage strategies or cronyism, distorting incentives and creating structural problems.

Delay of macroeconomic policy also tended to aggravate critical situations, rather than preventing further crisis. Before a crisis broke out, contractionary policy was introduced, but only after the adverse effect of the over-heated economy, or of the asset appreciation, had materialized. By the time the adverse effects are visible, the economy is already starting to slow down; thus, an expansionary, rather than a tight macroeconomic policy is needed. In Korea, however, a contractive policy has been adopted at this juncture, thus making the economy shrink rapidly. It has thus never been possible, however, for the contraction introduced to be promoted strongly enough or sustained long enough. This is because firms and banks have always asked for stimulus policies as production declined and profits decreased. Accordingly, immediately after the economic crises, governments had no choice but to relax macroeconomic policy. Pump-priming measures and favorable foreign economic conditions have then led to economic booms. This in turn sowed the seeds of a future crisis. Then, the story repeated itself.

Chapter 4

CHARACTERISTICS OF THE 1997 ECONOMIC CRISIS AND APPRAISAL OF ITS RESOLUTION

1. MAIN CHARACTERISTICS OF THE 1997 ECONOMIC CRISIS

The 1997 crisis differs from the previous ones in that the country could not resolve the critical situation with its own resources. There had been previous crises in which foreign debt had been the main problem, and in which the economy faced difficulty in inducing further capital inflow. At those times, however, the country had overcome the crises on the basis of its own creditworthiness. In 1997, in contrast, Korea could not borrow abroad any more. Thus, it had to depend on the liquidity facilities of international financial institutions and maturity rescheduling of foreign debts.

Another feature of the 1997 economic crisis is that even though the external shocks were weaker than those during the previous crises, e.g., the 1980 crisis, their effects were much stronger. As for the 1980 crisis, it was triggered by a number of large shocks. Externally, unstable international oil prices, turmoil in the international financial markets, and world-wide economic recession were all happening together. Internally, bad harvests were accompanied by political and social unrest. In 1997, however, the only shock was the instability in the international financial markets caused by the South East Asian currency crisis. The terms of trade had worsened in 1996, to a larger degree than expected, but they had then improved somewhat in 1997.

As for the impacts, that of the 1997 crisis seems to have been larger than that of the 1980 crisis, which was severe enough. The economic situations of 1980 and 1998 can be compared like this: in 1980, the growth rate was -2.1 percent and the unemployment rate 5.2 percent; in 1998, they were -6.7 percent and 6.8 percent, respectively. Moreover, the psychological impact seemed to be also larger in the 1997 crisis, because the crisis was a setback to Koreans who had taken such pride in the development of the Korean economy to join in the group of the advanced countries. The social impacts, such as damage to the middle and lower classes, were also huge.

The fact that the impact of the 1997 crisis was by far larger than those of other crises, even if the external shocks were relatively small, indicates that the main problem was weakness of the economic system as a whole. Of course, the extremely tight macroeconomic policy measures undertaken by the IMF program exacerbated the deep recession. However, the emergence of the crisis itself, even without any particularly large external shock, shows that the economic system was extremely fragile to shocks.

The extreme variety of types of crises involved in it may be another distinct feature of the 1997 crisis. Even though the 1980 crisis comprised many types of crisis factors, such as troubled firms, foreign debt-servicing problems, and inflation, it is analyzed as having been in essence a result of the simultaneous occurrence of external shocks. In the 1997 crisis, however, the sequence of events (firm insolvencies → non-performing loans of banks → loss of international confidence in the Korean economy) repeated itself twice or three times and generated corporate crisis, banking and/or financial crisis, and currency crisis in a series. To this list of crisis types might be added a balance of payments crisis, in that widening of current account deficits was one cause of those other types of crises. One trait of a policy-driven crisis may also be attached to the list, in that crisis resolution policy faltered over and again.

Considering the variety of features of the 1997 crisis, it seems to have resulted from all the problems remaining unresolved from past crises which all erupted at once by a relatively small shock from abroad. To put it another way, the innate problems of the Korean economic system finally came to greatly hinder the smooth operation of the economic system. The fact that a flaw in one sector could not be offset by the strength of another sector indicates that each part of the economic system was fragile. The variety of features of the 1997 economic crisis reflected these various weaknesses in almost all parts of the Korean economic system.

2. Comparison of the Structural Adjustment Policy since 1997 with the Past Economic Crisis Resolution

It appears too early to assess the policy responses to the 1997 crisis, since some of policy measures are in an ongoing process. In addition, its complexity would not allow an easy appraisal. One window to assess the recent crisis resolution measures may be provided, however, by comparison with the past crises. Compared with those adopted during past crises, the measures to cope with the 1997 crisis have some different aspects as well as some similar ones. Since most past crisis resolution measures were not effective, difference from them may be assessed as a positive feature, while similarity to past measures would be regarded as a negative feature of the recent structural adjustment policy. For example, the recent measures included an attempt to address the structural problems, something which was absent on past occasions. This can be evaluated as a positive feature.

A. Differences from the Previous Crisis Resolutions

The measures to resolve the 1997 crisis, unlike the previous ones, included attempts to provide indirect assistance to troubled firms and banks on the condition that they make their own efforts and take responsibility themselves to resolve their own problems. This differs from the unilateral provision of support in the previous crisis resolutions in that it has required the firms and banks being bailed-out to conduct restructuring. This is an improvement over the past crisis resolution measures, considering the fact that the past unilateral assistance tended to reduce the efficiency of the recipient firms and banks.

The recent crisis resolution policy also differs from the past ones in that the measures have spanned over a wide agenda and addressed fundamental issues. The measures included not only macroeconomic policy but also efforts to correct problems in the financial, corporate, labor, and public service sectors.

Another difference between the recent policy and earlier ones is that this time it addressed the issue of regulating the undesirable behavior of economic agent, for example, moral hazard, by adopting the global accounting standards and by strengthening the rule by law. This approach to curing the structural problems of the Korean economy should be highly evaluated.

The crisis resolution policy was so radical in a sense that it covered a wide-range agenda and touches the root causes of economic crisis. This was made possible by a social consensus, which was readily reached thanks to clear appearance of the structural problems as well as the wide-ranging impacts of the crisis.

The content of the policy was also different from those of previous ones in that it has included preemptive measures, to prevent recurrence of crisis, as well as *ex post* measures to cope with the troubled firms and banks. In the past, crisis resolution policy usually did not contain preventive measures. Nor was policy such as the clearance of non-performing loans of financial institutions promoted in a timely manner, right after the crisis breakout; rather, it tended to be implemented after the critical situation had somewhat calmed down. In contrast to this, the recent policy implemented the exits of insolvent banks and firms first, of all items on the agenda. Furthermore, policies taken at this time included changes in the laws and regulations, which was also *ex ante* in nature since it too aimed at preventing another crisis. Accordingly, the contents of the recent policy have also become different. In the past, the same policy tools as before were used again and again; in response to the 1997 crisis, however, new policy tools were adopted or old tools employed in different manners.

The mode of policy implementation this time changed to a radical reform or big-bang approach. This was because the government wanted to resolve the problems in many sectors within a short time span. Radical reform has the advantage of speeding up learning by all economic actors. It has the disadvantage, however, of requiring high adaptation costs. This contrasts to the gradual reform in the past, adopted mainly to reduce adaptation costs.

Another new feature in the recent crisis resolution is the improved variety and quality of policy instruments. In the past, financial instruments were almost the only measures used to cure any economic problem. In the 1997 crisis resolution, however, fiscal instruments and institutional rearrangements were added to the financial instruments, as new tools. Diversification of policy tools is meaningful; it has reminded policy makers that there are other policy tools than financial ones to achieve economic policy objectives.

In short, the 1997 crisis resolution policy can be highly evaluated in that it addressed the fundamental issues with various and wide-ranging policy tools.

Unlike the past ones, the recent structural adjustment policy has also attached more importance to the financial sector than to the real sector. Thus, the reform tends not to take the real sector's activities into account seriously. This is a cause for concern, because the source of long-run economic development in Korea has always been and still is in the real sector, and in the near future this situation does not seem likely to change dramatically; the Korean economy is still in the phase of economic development in which value is added mostly through industrial rather than financial competitiveness. In the increasingly competitive global environment, an economy is required to be very active in research and development in the real sector. Recently in Korea, however, investment has been extremely sluggish except in a few industries. This is partly because of the negligence of the structural adjustment programs in the real sectors.

B. Similarities to the Previous Crisis Resolutions

The 1997 crisis resolution policy also has some similarities with previous ones. Above all, it resembled past experience in that the government is playing a leading role in its design and implementation. The government first derived a consensus among workers and employers through the Tripartite Commission, and then promoted structural adjustment through the initiative of private actors. As time has gone by, however, the private sector agent's will to restructure has weakened, and in some cases the government has coercively pushed reforms to overrule disputes. Government initiation was certainly inevitable, because the reform was in its first stage (hardware reform) -- a stage in which resolution of the troubled firms and banks was the focal issue[1]. However, the government has not been able to proceed to the second stage reform (software reform).

Since the reform was mainly led by the government, the effects were expected to be limited. For example, although firms have sharply reduced their debt-equity ratios, as the government forced them to do so, this did not necessarily mean that they had quit their old ways of doing business; in fact, they lowered their ratios largely through the revaluation of assets and issue of new stocks, rather than by redeeming debts or selling assets.

The operation of macroeconomic policy during the recent crisis resolution process resembled the past, too. Just as in the previous cases, the stabilization policy implemented in the early stage of the crisis exacerbated the situation further. It does seem, however, that while the switch of macroeconomic policy from a restrictive to an expansionary base from mid-1998 was similar to the past in its timing, it was different in its purpose. It was done not so much to boost the economy, as it had been in the past, as to stop the troubles in firms and banks from spilling over to others. The policy seemed to have amplified the intensity of

---

[1] The government's intention to distinguish between the first stage structural adjustment (hardware reform), which attempts at introduction and establishment of formal institutions such as laws and regulations, and the second stage structural adjustment (software reform), which aims at changing the behaviors of individual actors, may be interpreted as having resulted from neglect of the fact that institutions comprise not only rules, but also behavioral patterns.

the business cycle because it was so strong in magnitude and was introduced in an environment characterized by greater uncertainty. It also misdirected or lessened the effects of the restructuring efforts.

3. Implications for Structural Adjustment Policy

The main lesson from the above analysis of four crises in the Korean economy is that the problems intrinsic to the economic system should be cured fundamentally so that a crisis does not recur. The 1997 economic crisis was caused by over-borrowings by firms, financial sector weakness, inefficiency in the economic system, and policy mistakes. All of these factors are fundamental problems of the Korean economy; they had all been causes for past crises. Mishandling of the problems in the past might have contributed to the 1997 crisis. Measures to prevent future crises should focus on resolving these fundamental problems[2].

In order to prevent the same problems causing further crises, the methods used in crisis resolution should be different in nature from those employed in the past. In the past, similar policies were repeatedly used, such as subsidizing distressed firms and financial institutions. These policies were not effective, as is shown by the recurrence of similar crises afterwards. In other words, to protect, to support, and to foster firms and banks just because they are core components of the economic system, is not an appropriate way to go. On the contrary, such a policy aggravates the fragility of the economic system. Therefore, a crisis resolution policy should avoid using such bail-out measures, in order to prevent a crisis from coming back. The fact that structural adjustment policy following the 1997 crisis did not use unilateral subsidies to troubled firms and financial institutions should be highly evaluated.

It should also be noted that the measures initiated by the government, including the introduction of new laws and guidelines to improve the financial structures of firms and financial institutions, are not sufficient to prevent reoccurrence of a crisis. The measures so far were undertaken to establish the proper environment to enable firms and financial institutions to do business in a changed manner. The undertaking of such measures is one thing, and whether the firms and financial institutions will actually change their behavior is another.

[2] That an economic crisis may happen because of factors other than those so far discussed remains a possibility, of course.

Firms and financial institutions should reinforce their business competence by themselves, lest they confront crisis again.

All economic agents, including firms and financial institutions, stakeholders, and the government, should make efforts together in order to complete the structural adjustment policy successfully. Above all, firms and banks must put their efforts into reducing their structural weaknesses. Moreover, the roles of stockholders, employees, creditors and customers, in checking and monitoring the behavior of firms or financial institutions, should also be strengthened. In addition, the government should enact regulations and laws ensuring that firms and financial institutions operate on their own initiative and exert their creativeness freely, and that they also assume responsibilities consonant with their new freedom to choose.

In this respect, introduction and implementation of the concept of the so-called second-generation reform is necessary for the success of the second stage structural adjustment policy. While the first-generation reform typically involves liberalization, stabilization, and selected structural reforms, the second-generation reform focuses on deeper and broader institutional reform, to enhance institutional capabilities (World Bank 1997). The first-generation reform can mostly be enacted through executive order, and thus the main actors are limited to the few elite technocrats. The second-generation reform, however, relates to all those affected by the institutional change. This implies that the government should refrain from initiating reforms, and ways should be opened for all interested parties to participate in the reform process, i.e., in identifying the problems, improving institutions, and creating a new economic order, all with the willingness for mutual understanding and compromise.

Macroeconomic policy, moreover, as a part of the crisis prevention measures, should be implemented in a manner different from the past. It is the timing of a stabilization policy that matters. In the past, poor timing of stabilization policy typically lessened the effects of stabilization policy. Stabilization measures were introduced just when the economy had begun to stagnate after a long period of boom, and seldom contributed to preventing recurrence of crisis. If a stabilization policy is to be used, it should be implemented in a preemptive manner so that it can prevent an exceptional boom or wide-spread speculation, which is one of the main macroeconomic causes of an economic crisis. Even in that case, of course, the authorities must remember that microeconomic means to reduce corporate over-borrowings and restrain banks' exposures are no less important in achieving the purpose than aggregate demand management

Chapter 5

TENTATIVE CONCLUSION

This book employed an approach different from those lying behind the various common views of the recent structural adjustment policy in Korea. This book has first defined structural adjustment policy as a set of measures to prevent economic crisis from recurring, and then evaluated the effectiveness of the crisis resolution measures from this perspective. Utilization of this approach could probably do away with the confusions, which have arisen, among various reasons, from lack of a consistent analytic framework.

Another feature of this book is that it has attempted at finding some ways to enhance the effectiveness of the structural adjustment policy, based on analysis and comparison of past experiences. The successes or failures in past attempts at crisis resolution should be of great help in evaluating the recent one, considering the fact that there is no complete theory or experimentation on what constitutes an ideal restructuring program.

Finally, it should also be noted that historic facts are subject to different interpretations, depending upon what point of view they are seen from. The same is true of the interpretation of the ongoing Korean economic structural adjustment policy. A researcher may arrive at different conclusions or draw different policy implications from those contained in this book if he starts from a different point of view. Therefore, more effective assessment of the structural adjustment policy would entail analyses from many points of view, and then a synthesis of them.

Bearing all of these points in minds, this book can reach a tentative conclusion as follows: Korea has experienced four episodes of economic crisis since the 1960s. This book examined each crisis and found out that the same factors that caused one previous crisis later brought about another crisis repeatedly. This implies that the measures taken to resolve the previous crises were ultimately ineffective. Most of the past crisis resolution measures focused on disposing of the losses incurred by firms and banks through such instruments as bail-out loans. As far as macroeconomic policy is concerned, stabilization measures were introduced just when the economy had begun to stagnate after a long period of boom, and seldom contributed to preventing recurrence of crisis; rather, they amplified the crisis intensity.

These results suggest several lessons for the restructuring policy. First, it should be designed in such a way as to encourage private agents to take initiative, with the government abstaining from direct intervention such as bail-out loans. This would eventually strengthen private sector capacity to overcome adverse shocks. Second, if a stabilization policy is to be used, it should be implemented in a preemptive manner, so that it can prevent an excessive boom or wide-spread speculation.

REFERENCES

(IN KOREAN)

The Bank of Korea, (1973). A *Comprehensive Report on The August 3rd Economic Emergency Decree,* Seoul: The Bank of Korea.

____, *Economic Statistics Yearbook*, various issues.

____, *National Account*, various issues.

____, *Financial Statement Analysis*, various issues.

____, (1998). *Statistical Yearbook of Foreign Exchange*, Seoul: The Bank of Korea.

____, (2000). *The Bank of Korea: A History of Fifty Years*, Seoul: The Bank of Korea.

Economic Planning Board, (1980). *Economic Policy in the Periods of Liberalized and Open Economy: 30 Years of the Economic Planning Board II*, Seoul: Economic Planning Board.

Fair Trade Commission, *Fair Trade White Book*, various issues.

Kim, Jung-Ryum, (1990). *30 Years of Economic Development Policy in Korea: Memoirs of Kim Jung-Ryum*, Seoul: Jungang Ilbo

Korea Development Institute, (1981). *Collections of Economic Stabilization Policy Measures (Book I and Book II)*, Seoul: Korea Development Institute.

Lee, Jong Kyu, (2000). Economic Crisis: Causes and Genetic Process, *Economic Studies Series,* No. 2, Seoul: Economic Studies Office, The Bank of Korea.

(IN ENGLISH)

Fry, Maxwell J., (1995). *Money Interest, and Banking in Economic Development* (2nd Ed.), Baltimore and London: Johns Hopkins University Press.

Goldstein, Morris and Philip Turner, (1996). Banking Crises in Emerging Economies: Origins and Policy Options," *BIS Economic Papers*, No. 46, Basle, Switzerland: Bank for International Settlements.

IMF, (1997). Republic of Korea - Request for Stand-by Arrangement, mimeograph.

Kang, David, (2002). Bad Loans to Good Friends: Money Politics and the Development State in South Korea, *International Organization 56*, 177-207.

Kindleberger, Charles P., (1996). *Manias, Panics and Crises: A History of Financial Crises*, 3rd edition, New York: John Wiley and Sons.

Krueger, Anne O., (1993). *Political Economy of Policy Reform in Developing Countries*, Cambridge: MIT Press.

Lee, S. and K. Cheong, (2007). The Political Economy of Financial Structure of Korean Firms, *Journal of Developing Areas*, forthcoming.

MacKinnon, Ronald I., (1973). *Money and Capital in Economic Development*, Washington D. C.: Brookings Institution.

Schandler, Susan et al., (1995). *IMF Conditionality: Experience under Stand-by and Extended Arrangements, Part I: Key Issues and Findings*, IMF Occasional Paper, No. 128, Washington D. C.: IMF.

World Bank, (1997). *The State in a Changing World*, World Development Report 1997, New York: Oxford University Press.

INDEX

A

B

C

D

E

F

G

H

I

J

K

L

M

N

O

P